ACP0680

PEDAGOGY
OF THE HEART

PAULO FREIRE

PEDAGOGY OF THE HEART

Notes by Ana Maria Araújo Freire

---

*Translated by Donaldo Macedo
and Alexandre Oliveira*

Foreword by Martin Carnoy
Preface by Ladislau Dowbor

CONTINUUM · NEW YORK

1998

The Continuum Publishing Company
370 Lexington Avenue
New York, NY 10017

Copyright © 1997 by Ana Maria Araújo Freire

Printed in the United States of America

Library of Congress Cataloging-in-Publication Data

Freire, Paulo, 1921–
[A sombra desta mangueira. English]
Pedagogy of the heart / Paulo Freire ; notes by
Ana Maria Araújo Freire ; translated by Donaldo Macedo and
Alexandre Oliveira ; foreword by Martin Carnoy.
p.   cm.
Includes bibliographical references (p.   ).
ISBN 0-8264-1131-2 (pbk.)   : alk. paper
1. Politics and education.   2. Popular education.
3. Politics and education—Brazil.   4. Popular education—Brazil.
I. Freire, Ana Maria Araújo, 1933–   . II. Title.
LC71.F7413   1997
370.11'5—dc21   97-15797
                                                        CIP

Contents

Foreword

BY MARTIN CARNOY, STANFORD UNIVERSITY

The late Paulo Freire was the most important educator of the second half of this century. He was also a political activist—a passionate progressive who believed in the inseparability of learning from political consciousness and of political consciousness from political action.

In this book, Paulo Freire looks into his own life to reflect on education and politics, politics and education. He reveals himself as an uncompromising democrat and unrepentant radical reformer. He lived through military rule, exile, and even the holding of political power as São Paulo's Secretary of Education. In that office, he made policy for the education of hundreds of thousands of pupils. All of these experiences have only increased his commitment to the excluded, the powerless, the marginalized, the hungry, the illiterate.

Much of the book is about Brazil and particular issues of Brazilian politics. Brazil is in many ways unique. One of the great new industrial economies, enormously wealthy and enormously poor, it has the most unequal income distribution of any of the world's major countries. Its political system, multiparty and highly democratic at one level, is still run on the basis of *clientelismo*, in which politicians maintain power by using public resources for very specific private interests. And, although as Freire argues, the educational system is now internally democratic in many municipalities, it is one of the most stratified and least accessible in Latin America. Even with rapid enrollment growth in the past ten years, only about one-third of fifteen-to-nineteen-year-olds attend secondary school. Teachers' salaries have fallen drastically during that same period (as in much of the rest of Latin America), and the conditions in basic education are desperately poor.

Even if Paulo Freire was first and foremost Brazilian, or even more particularly, a Northeast Brazilian, from the cradle of Luso-Afro-American civilization, his ideas are in the world and from the world. He is an anomaly among educators because he is truly international. He is as well known in Nicaragua or in France as he is in Brazil. He also has an enormous following in the United States, not just among intellectuals but among primary school teachers and adult educators.

So his Brazilian thoughts address worldly issues. We in the North need to pay much greater attention to them. For better or worse, we have entered the global age and we entered it together with Paulo Freire, the Brazilian *Nordestino*, sitting in the shade of his mango tree.* Our social condition may appear to be altogether different, but as we push below the surface of our everyday lives, we find that the questions we are asking ourselves require the same larger considerations. Freire addresses progressives everywhere, urging them to remain active, authentic, democratic, nonsectarian, and unifying. But to do this, he argues, progressives must continuously examine their underlying strategies. New conditions demand new answers to some of the same old difficult questions: What is the role of a progressive politics in the world system, now a new global-information economy? What is the role of progressive intellectuals? And what is the role of democratic education, again now in the information age? These are questions just as fundamental to those who want progressive change in the North as they are to Paulo Freire.

What are these new conditions? The first is that world economy has changed profoundly in the past generation. It has be-

---

*The original title of this book is *À Sombra desta Mangueira*, translated as "under the shade of this mango tree."

come *globalized.* Globalization does not simply mean international trade and movements of capital and labor. In that sense, the economy has always been global. The recent change represents a profound shift of economic time and space, from the local and national into the global arena. A communications and information revolution has made this shift possible, but so has the spread of lower-tech industrial technology, education, and large accumulations of capital to areas outside of the United States/Europe axis. Production is less and less conducted in one location or even in one country. Capital *and* labor *and* knowledge are increasingly conceived of in global terms. Whatever the powerful role of capital flows in influencing national development in the past, these have been expanded, particularly in the speed by which capital can move from country to country, and by the very *size* of the movements.

The globalization of national and local economies is changing the underlying basis of the nation–state. The capitalist nation–state in the period of agricultural expansion and industrialization was largely defined in terms of the boundaries of its national raw-material base, national industries, and national market. To expand economic and political control, nations had to occupy more territory. Losing economic and political control meant losing territory. That definition is changing very quickly. As globalization changes the concept of economic time and space, the political control vested in national territories changes. Nation–states still have a role in influencing the course of their development. They also have a range of policy choices framed by political forces. We can see this in the variety of approaches to capitalist development found among highly industrialized countries. But the increased competition for capital and for goods and services made possible partly by the information and communications revolution has changed the conditions and possibilities for national policies. National (and local) politics today is increasingly constrained to *shaping the culture of global capitalism as it is manifested nationally and locally.* Economic globalization means the globalization of local social movements. Local politics means the localization of global capitalism. Local becomes global and global becomes local.

Modern politics has always been intertwined with economic production. When capitalist states are inflexible, inefficient, and obsolete, they drag down their economies. When production systems have difficulty changing, they drag down their states. This is not only the case for countries such as Brazil and Mexico, it is also true for us in the North. But what does it mean for a state to be "flexible" and "efficient" in the information age? This is a fundamental political question for national and local politics. It is also the basic issue in defining authentic national and local culture in the global-information age.

Neoliberals and progressives seem to agree on one major criterion for a flexible and efficient state. It must be democratic, where the measure of democracy if free and open elections, including all adult citizens as voters regardless of gender, race, or ethnicity. This constitutes a second major new condition, both for the left and the right. In the past, neoliberals easily opted for the authoritarian state to ensure unconditional capitalist control of capital accumulation, even when the democratic decision was to restrict that control. Progressives also easily rationalized authoritarianism to maintain control of the process of capital accumulation in the hands of the state, even when elections would have decided otherwise.

But for all their new agreement on the principal of democracy, neoliberals and progressives have a fundamental disagreement about the *meaning* of the democratic state. For neoliberals, flexibility and efficiency mean a minimalist state that allows business maximum freedom to accumulate capital; this on the assumption that unfettered capital accumulation will produce maximum economic growth and the greatest social good. The neoliberal model for national and local culture subordinates them to the needs of the global market, to individual competition in an isolated, Darwinian struggle for survival. Competition is not just local or even national. It is global. Brazilian capital competes against French; workers in São Paulo against workers in Shanghi. The neoliberal state is left to facilitate competition and to educate labor for competition in a global environment. Education is measured in terms of students' ability to score as well on mathematics tests as pupils in Korea or Japan or Germany.

For Freire, the flexible and efficient state in the information age is very different. It helps its constituents become critical activists shaping the economy and society into a humane, participative system that accumulates capital but not in an exploitative, highly unequal fashion. The efficient state is also one that protects its citizens against the risks and excesses of a free market. This contrasts sharply with the "incomplete" democratic politics of neoliberalism—a politics reduced to enhancing isolated individuals' solitary competitiveness in a Darwinian struggle. Freire's state is *constructive*, one where citizens are reintegrated through forming new political and social networks based both on information *and* critical analysis of their own situation in the global environment. Freire's state is also one of *solidarity*, including the marginalized, even when the global market has no room for them and exclusionary local ideologies segregate them.

How can the solidarity state hope to keep domestic capital from flying off into the ether of the global flows? How can such a state, rooted in the empowerment of citizens and workers, hope to attract international technology transfer and capital investment? Neoliberals argue that it cannot; that it would *inherently* drive capital and new technology away. But with Paulo Freire at our side, let us consider this carefully. Capital needs a stable political environment for high returns over the long term. Stability is impossible in societies marked by great income and information inequality, uneven participation, exclusion, and the absence of a critically aware citizenry that is prepared to solve political problems in its own interest. Political and social stability needs *reintegration* of isolated individuals so as to create a new collective will, what some analysts have called *social capital*. Capital also needs flexible workers, and to be flexible, workers need families and social institutions that are integrative, capable of building and sustaining educational as well as training networks, and supporting workers, in periods of unemployment and training. These are precisely what the solidarity state delivers. Democratic, progressive states that aim to create more equal distribution of income and reintegrative, participative social institutions with an eye to promoting savings, capital investment, and human capital development, are fundamental to high productivity growth and reasonably high long-term rates of return to capital. This is neither the welfare state nor the neoliberal state; it is new form of reintegrative state.

Nowhere in Freire's answer to the neoliberal view of the state do we find a critique of participating in democratic elections. This is no accident. That ancient debate between Kautsky and Lenin about whether elections are a means for revolutionary workers to gain control of the capitalist state (Kautsky) or nothing more than a bourgeois "trick" to co-opt the revolution (Lenin) is relegated to the historical archives. Freire's position is centered in the democratic, antimilitary movements of the 1970s and 1980s. Participation in elections is a hard-won right belonging as much to workers and peasants as to the bourgeoisie. Thus, the role of a progressive political party goes beyond Gramsci's counterhegemonical, or "educational" function. Freire's conception of a progressive party is educational in the Gramscian tradition. Yet, it is also a means to strengthening democracy, to gaining political power, and to advancing its social objectives through the democratic but still market-supporting state. Having achieved a transition to democracy, Freire writes, the left in Brazil now enters another political phase: *intimacy* with democracy, living with it and deepening it so that it has real meaning in people's everyday lives.

But it is fair to ask what happens to a progressive party in the context of the new globalization and the new democracy, especially when the party gains power. Freire argues that to retain its authenticity, a party of the left needs constantly to open itself to dialogue, to change. This is precisely the historical moment for such questioning. Is globalized capital so powerful that the state is limited to the neoliberal agenda? Freire says no. He believed that even as capital circulates in global space, it must land somewhere to realize profits. A progressive transformation of the state need not overthrow the market or capital accumulation per se to humanize economy and society. The solidarity state can provide the basis of a more flexible, competitive, and innovative economy by developing the new reintegrative networks required for workers and families in the information age. Yet these networks need to be developed on terms that represent the interests of workers, the poor, the old, the excluded—not just capital's needs.

Does globalization in the information age put new limits on what the state can transform, especially at the national level? This is a more difficult question. To accomplish its goals, a progressive political party needs to develop local and national politics that are consistent with the social and economic changes wrought locally by the globalized economy. Worldwide neoliberal ideology attempts to define the limits of those politics. However, as Freire put it so well, (in Brazil) the left, whether it be in the form of left party or in the form of the current progressive-intellectual leadership of a center-right coalition, has to go beyond the limits of the neoliberal definition to develop its own conditions of capitalist development. The impetus for pushing beyond the limits of the neoliberal definition worldwide has to come from social movements associated with political parties and alliances, whether it be left parties in Brazil or labor unions in France. All of these local struggles of definition are struggles over the *culture of global capital* in the information age.

Strategies for defining the new limits for flexible and efficient states are necessarily localized in national and local realities. Surprisingly, there are similarities among realities in Europe, the United States, and Brazil. One of these was especially important for Freire and the Brazilian left: the current president of Brazil is one of the world's leading progressive intellectuals and a brilliant political thinker and strategist: Fernando Henrique Cardoso. Cardoso heads a "center-right" coalition. From the standpoint of Brazil's major left party, Freire's Workers' Party (PT), Cardoso has abandoned his progressive ideals and is working well within the neoliberal definition of the state's role in the new global economy. But the outcome of the Cardoso regime is hardly clear. Education enrollment is expanding rapidly, and the democratizing educational policies pushed by PT-run and other local administrations are being supported rather than opposed at the national level. Furthermore, Cardoso appears committed to a strategy of deepening democracy—of refashioning the political involvement of the great mass of the Brazilian poor and marginalized—as a means of eventually redefining the culture of Brazilian capitalism. Is this a mistaken strategy in a country where the process of capital accumulation has long been at the mercy of particular interests within and outside the country? Is it a mistake to solidify democratic political stability, undo the debt-driven economic chaos of the 1980s, and build the base for a new social policy in the next millennium? Consistent with his own intellectual openness, Freire does not completely turn the page on this chapter of Brazilian history. Freire *and* Cardoso both knew that Brazil's economic and political future depends on greater equality of income and wealth. Cardoso believes that Brazil needs first to grow more confident of its economic future and to expand political participation even if the tilt toward neoliberal economic-stabilization policies delays equalization. Freire believed that the very *process* of equalization is needed to develop the new Brazilian economy outside the suffocating confines of global neoliberalism. Is there any wonder that Brazil's progressive intellectuals are divided on which strategy is "correct"?

Similar discussions are taking place in other countries, under political circumstances that are very different. The United States should hardly be lacking confidence in its economic future. But in the new global environment, buffeted by competition from Asia and the flight of its domestic industry abroad, by corporate downsizing, stagnant wages, and a disintegrating system of social support, United States workers are afraid. The successful onslaught of neoliberal ideology and a growing distrust of politicians has converted those fears into a "flight from the state." In this environment, President Clinton has, like Fernando Henrique Cardoso, tilted toward economic policies that would reassure finance capital, and toward social "investment" policies that focus on education to rebuild public confidence in the state. Is this strategy a wrong one? Many progressive intellectuals in the United States believe so. But unlike Brazil, there is no progressive political party or parties where alternative strategies can develop and be presented to the public. The progressive wing of the Democratic Party would have to reorganize itself and rebuild its base (using the increasingly active labor unions and newly reawakened civil-rights organizations), to push Clinton toward a broader, deeper social agenda. Without that push, neoliberals will continue to win the battle over the culture of American capitalism, and in winning that battle, to shape similar battles in other countries, including the nations of Europe and Brazil.

In Italy, Romano Prodi heads the first center-left coalition to govern the country. But Italy is part of the new Europe, and Europe is reshaping itself as a regional economic power, the better to compete in the new global economy. Prodi's government is confronted by the conditions of the Maastricht Treaty (monetary union), which include stringent reductions in public debt and public deficits. The reductions, driven by a conservative German definition of healthy economic policy are inherently contractionary. They necessarily require a reduction of the social safety net and possibly reduction of educational spending, this in an Italy that desperately needs to invest in expanding and raising the quality of its university system. Prodi's situation reinforces the notion that even a center-left coalition, led by political parties opposed to a neoliberal conception of the state, in a country where a large part of the electorate continues to believe in activist state intervention and social policies, faces powerful economic and ideological forces that dominate the coalition's strategies and policies.

What do progressives—especially activist progressive intellectuals—need to focus on in the new context? Freire puts it well in these pages: push against limits, create space, redefine the social agenda. In Freire's "intimacy" with democracy, the struggle is at least partly ideological. He exhorts us to think of political strategies and state policies that will humanize the culture of global capital as it lands in our locality. But the struggle is not only ideological. Social policy has real economic and social consequences for the poor and marginalized, *and* for the rich and the middle class. The consequences are not just symbolic. They shape people's lives and their place in the material world.

In no social policy has the new global information economy made Freire more relevant than in education. Freire has redefined the political meaning of education and recast the underlying struggle over education. For him, education has the potential to be liberating, and liberating education is the path to knowledge and critical thinking. Knowledge is the foundation of the new global information economy. Globalization has enhanced the importance of knowledge, of innovativeness, of critical thinking, and the capacity to solve problems. Economic progress in any country increasingly requires a broad base of highly conscious, self-confidant, critical-thinking, participative, literate, and numerate individuals to compete in the new world economy.

Beyond that, as businesses restructure to be more productive, they are moving away from Fordist, assembly-line industrial production to *flexible* work organizations. Flexibility can mean many things. But its essential elements are the capacity to adjust quickly to changes in product demand and production technology. The up side is that in firms that focus on raising productivity, flexibility has meant the opportunity for workers to engage in multiple tasks and more interesting work, and to feel empowered. The down side is that many firms see flexibility in terms of lowering labor costs—to increase some workers' opportunities, to rid themselves more easily of others, and to make all jobs subject to potential elimination. Both these forms of flexibility disaggregate labor from the "job" as a permanent source of income and self-definition. The worker is individualized, separated from traditional social organizations based on the worker's job or workplace, and made to rely on his or her acquired capacity to adjust to change, to participate in diverse productive activities, and to be independent and creative.

Paulo Freire's thoughts on education in these pages as elsewhere speak to this transformation at several levels. Education that *works effectively* to keep poor children in school and learning is absolutely essential to the notion of flexible production. Freire's work as Secretary of Education in São Paulo was all about making the educational process meaningful for teachers and pupils in low-income schools, and through this meaning to enhance learning and keep children in school. *Conscientização* is the essential ingredient of developing such meaning. Freire's conception of education is also essential to flexibility in Freire's focus on critical thinking, the development of self- and collective-identity, democratic participation, and cooperation. In many studies of what employers value most in "high performance" organizations, these are precisely the characteristics that head the list. And finally, Freire thinks of critical education as a form of networking—a "community" of knowledge and knowledge formation. New networks are also essential to flexibility and productivity. As families and traditional, stable neighborhoods disintegrate under the onslaught of flexible production, new networks are needed to reproduce skills and knowledge. It is this new and, in many ways, virtual community that could replace traditional job-based social networks and residential neighborhoods. Freire envisages the political party as the major form of this critical-knowledge community, but the traditional political party is also being transformed by the new information and communication environment. Television, for example, has already made drastic changes, deconstructing the traditional political party apparatus and the use of critical knowledge in politics. Yet, Freire's knowledge of communities could be the basis for new kinds of networks beyond the traditional political party, networks formed around schools and adult education, youth organizations, and religious organizations with a common interest to enhance individual and collective value.

This list makes clear how far neoliberals can stay on Freire's education train, and where they have to get off. They are certainly comfortable with expanding schooling and making it more effective. In the great competitiveness debates now circling the globe, higher test scores and low dropout rates are the currency of postmodern economies. In other words, *conscientização* could well be the centerpiece of a neoliberal educational policy if it enhances learning, keeps children in school, and makes schooling resources more effective. To some degree, Freire's focus on critical thinking is also acceptable to neoliberals, especially in countries where business ideology is powerful enough to harness critical thinking to the needs of mainstream private business-based activities.

But now consider the meaning of Freire's critical education in a society with a more contested culture of capital. Neoliberals would not be willing to take the risk. In a contested culture, the networks emerging from the critical construction of knowledge would likely enter into developing a new culture of capital. This is what Freire envisages, and this is where neoliberals retreat from effective, inclusive, democratic, problem-solving education.

Thus, Freire exposes a major contradiction of the neoliberal model in the information age. The basis for economic and social development in the new global economy is conscious critical thinking and knowledge networks. For more than thirty years, Paulo Freire thought about the revolutionary nature of knowledge. The needs of global capitalists have caught up with his conception of education. But once there, they cannot unilaterally incorporate its participative democratic implications. Freire understood this. The new knowledge networks, both as the reintegrators of disaggregated workers and as sites of continuing education and *conscientização*, could serve to shape the future nature of local and national politics, and from there, the nature of global capital.

Preface

BY LADISLAU DOWBOR

Writing a preface for a book by Paulo Freire gives one the strange sensation of being redundant. In his characteristic style, Paulo does not simply write; he *thinks* his act of writing through as well, in a permanent distancing from himself. What is left for the preface writer to do is to recover the image in the mirror, and the image's image.

What is even stranger is for such a task to be bestowed on a professional in the field of economics, which, probably more than any other, was responsible for a dominant theoretical framework where concerns with ethics, solidarity, and simple emotions such as happiness and personal satisfaction disappear. The dry legacy inherited from Jeremy Bentham and Stuart Mill is *utilitarianism,* the rather cynical notion that it is enough for each individual to maximize his or her profit in order that a world can be obtained which is not socially ideal, but which is the best possible.

The "thirty golden years" that followed the end of World War II saw an impressive capitalist productive explosion. Undoubtedly, this explosion has led many to believe that profit-driven capitalists, who develop production, indeed do more for the poor than the lefts who clamor for justice. This trend became even stronger when the authoritarian socialism alternative went down: only one option was left on the table, the necessary evil, capitalism.

History reduced to economic mechanisms and all values subsumed by the realism of individual advantage, conscience-bearing humanity felt cornered into a pragmatic form of fatalism decorating their day-to-day lives with increasingly absurd technological junk while trying to reconstruct their horizon of viable utopias.

This rebuilding is necessary and most comprehensive; it involves the very conceptualizing of the civilization we wish to build. And, even if the different directions in this accelerated process of transformation are hard to predict, some parameters are becoming most clear.

One central parameter is provided by the current technological explosion. In the past twenty years, we have accumulated more technological knowledge than in the entire history of humanity. Human beings handle potent agropesticides, nuclear and bacteriological weapons, sophisticated systems for genetic manipulation, industrial fishing fleets with advanced technology for locating schools of fish, fine chemistry processes that allow for the back-alley production of both advanced medication and cocaine or heroine. In the meantime, human capacity for government has evolved extremely slowly.

The result of such a society that transforms itself while following different rhythms is that human beings are handling technologies far more advanced than their own political maturity. This fact is ascertained by the destruction of life in rivers and in the ocean, by ozone depletion, by the increased use of drugs, and by the availability of sophisticated systems of destruction available to any would-be terrorist. Humanity will not survive without more advanced forms of social organization, ones capable of surpassing this articulated chaos of corporate interests that we have come to call *neoliberalism*, and that manages technology of irreversible, universal impact.

Another important parameter is the deep transformation that occurred in spaces for social reproduction. Economies have become internationalized for the largest part, while instruments for social control have remained national. As a result, for example, nobody controls the nearly $1 trillion*

---

*All dollar figures are U.S., unless otherwise noted.

circulating daily in global financial spaces. Likewise, there is no organized power structure capable of organizing any effective compensation for the nearly $500 billion annually transferred from poor to rich countries. On another level, society has become widely urbanized, but decisions remain in the hands of central governments, much like the time when nations consisted of "capitals" surrounded by dispersed rural populations. Urbanization threw the problem over to the cities, which are in the front-line of difficulties but at the base of the power pyramid. The political world has become an impressive web of institutions that have to make decisions about what they do not know, and that have no decision-making power over the realities with which they are, in effect, faced. Today, it is our very conceptualization over the organizational hierarchy of political power that must be rethought, aiming at returning the reins of its own development to society.

Within such an environment of lost governability, the megastructures of the end of this century prosper: large transnational corporations, initially focused on productive sectors, are equally dominant today in the dynamic environments of service and finance. Today, about five to six hundred companies control 25 percent of world production, dominate in the most technologically dynamic areas, and mold the world to the demands of competition. There is little opportunity within corporate strategy for reflection upon the social or environmental interests of humanity. As a result of reengineering, total quality, ISO-9000, robotics, telecomputing, benchmarking, and so many other magic words that promise effectiveness and efficiency, lean-and-mean capitalism, compelled by the very rules of efficiency, is leaving little room for reflecting upon values. It is curious to see the pope of American business administration, Peter Drucker, write a book, in the midst of the communist collapse, titled *Post-Capitalist Society*, seeking the construction of a community "based on commitment and compassion."

This modernity, whose technologic innovations fill us with awe, gives very little sense of commitment or compassion.

While eight hundred million people in rich countries enjoy an ostentatious $20,000 per-capita income, 3.2 billion dwellers of the underdeveloped world live on an average of $350, less than $30 a month. Today, about one hundred fifty million children starve in the world, a statistic projected for one hundred eighty million by the year 2000, while some twelve million simply die before the age of five. Illiteracy affects more than eight hundred million people, and this number increases by about ten million each year. Close to ninety million new inhabitants come into the world annually, about sixty million of whom are born into the most destitute areas, condemned on their first day of life. They cannot manage the fifty cents per child that they would need for iodine, to prevent goiter, or the ten cents for vitamin A to prevent blindness. About one million children become mutilated for life every year. Half a million mothers die in labor every year for not having access to basic medical information and services: in all the rich countries combined, this number is only five thousand. A devastated Africa cries the loss of its last trees and sees its unprotected soil taken away by the wind and by pouring rains, while the West, which has devastated it, recommends that it care for its environment. But each day we have better and better computers, VCRs, and CD players.

It is unnecessary to keep multiplying the examples. The important thing is that the time is running out when humanity can rely on spontaneous "mechanisms," on *laissez-faire*, *laissez-passer*, without defining itself as a civilization.

A first obvious realization is that capitalism constitutes an excellent environment for making production more dynamic, but it has yet to learn how to create effective distribution mechanisms. In reality, the very power struggle generated by privileges and by the accumulation of wealth by minorities prevents a balanced distribution. It is not hard to predict that a planet that is becoming smaller and smaller each day, due to advances in transportation and communications, cannot live with increasingly dramatic economic polarization.

We realize, at the end of this century, that it is quite simply a theoretical error to predict a certain ethics of privilege, the notion that the accumulation of wealth by the rich would lead to more investments, more jobs, more production, and finally, more prosperity for all, along the lines of the infamous trickle-down effect. To the extent that there is a certain gap between the rich and the poor, markets become segmented, and a large part of the world's population is simply kept at the margin of the central process of wealth accumulation led by transnational corporations. The end of all hope for trickling down means that, structurally speaking, neoliberalism does not respond to modern challenges. It is necessary to seek new solutions.

Finally, the very core of capitalist theory—that the maximization of individual interests will guarantee the best social interests—is negated by the facts. At this stage of global capitalism, compensatory social policies by governments are insufficient not only in the countries bearing the negative onus for current development models, but also in developed countries, where people are tired of living under the terror of unemployment or of killing themselves working for objectives that are in doubtful relation to quality of life.

Rather than the search for a more effective way of doing the same, what is coming on strong now is a redefinition of the search itself. Gradually, through insecure approaches, we are seeking to reinsert values, ethics, and objectives into the dynamics of social reproduction. And this leads us to rethink the social agents capable of bringing about transformations and mobilization strategies.

In part, this is the path that leads an economist who realizes that the problems within his field call for solutions belonging to a broader universe onto the same discussion platform as that of an educator, who also looks for answers in the economic, social, and political realms. After all, the challenge posed by the end of this century is the question of our common future.

Pedagogy of the Heart, in the original Portuguese entitled "under this mango tree," perhaps more so than Paulo Freire's other books, presents an explicit view of the world, of politics, and of values. It considers, in the most positive sense, building bridges and pathways amid the smells and tastes of childhood, forming and transforming education, modern-world technological dynamics, economic injustice and absurdity, the search for political alternatives, and the personal commitment implied by that search, returning to the mango tree as the source of an identity that rediscovers and re-creates itself.

The source is essential here, for while we are still intoxicated with technological innovations, it brings us back to our real objectives, as human beings. Hypnotized by little pocket mirrors, more and more we perceive capitalism as the generator of scarcity: while the volume of technological toys available in stores increases, clean rivers for fishing and swimming, tree-shaded yards, clean air, clean drinking water, streets for playing or walking around, fruits eaten without fear of chemicals, free time, and spaces for informal socialization become more and more scarce. Capitalism requires that free-of-charge happiness be substituted for what can be bought and sold.

The alternative is not being against technology, as Milton Friedman would have it, when he states that all concerned with the environment and social causes have "progress-phobia" as a common trait. Any person with common sense understands how absurd it is for us to spend hours of our lives in city traffic, breathing polluted air, bumper to bumper, wasting oil, parts, pavement, health, and time, traveling at an average speed lower than ten miles per hour, slower than carriages from the turn of the century. The automobile is great, but only when inserted in a view of technology directed toward an enhanced quality of life, with a high priority for comfortable and affordable public transportation, tree-shaded streets, and individual transportation reserved for medium-length weekend trips or for large purchases.

Capitalism does not bring us only product, but also forms of social organization that destroy our ability to use it adequately. We powerlessly watch the stupefaction of children and adults in front of the television and the fact that we spend more and more time intensely working to buy more things designed to save us time. By the same token, we see the amazing advancement of available potential, and we are unable to turn it into a better life.

Indeed, a better life includes access to better things, but it also includes, and fundamentally so, the ensuing human relations. It is not very difficult to invert Sartre's sentence and state that happiness lies within others. In large part, more-or-less artificial political divisions touch on this generally nonexplicit belief that man is either naturally good or naturally evil. Today, we know the extent to which contexts that pitch man against man generate hell, whereas contexts that generate solidarity build environments where people feel more fulfilled.

A reordering of spaces for social reproduction has everything to do with this process. In the fortunate expression of Milton Santos, "That which is global divides; it is the local that allows for union." This century-and-a-half of capitalism has disjointed communities and created a truly anonymous society, whose members only interact through functional systems and electronic terminals. How to rebuild solidarity is the radical objective of Paulo Freire's reasoning.

We are all used to the conscience blow we take when we walk past street children. We have already built our defenses, one way or another. A long time ago, I met an elderly lady begging for money and was astounded by her resemblance to my mother. That was a deep shock, but then I was surprised with myself: "The anonymous human being is not supposed to hurt?" With the global society of long distances and large numbers, solidarity became no longer a matter of the heart, of feelings naturally generated before the known person; it shifted over to the intellect, reason, which is satisfied with rationalization. That which globalizes divides, and the pathway to solutions has to go through a deep rearticulation of the social fabric.

In Paulo Freire's reasoning, rationality is rationally clamoring for the right to its emotional roots. This is the return to the shade of the mango tree, to the complete human being. And with the smells and tastes of childhood, it is much broader a concept than that of right or left, a deeply radical one: human solidarity.

Under the Shade
of a Mango Tree

Solitude–Communion

The search that brings me to the comforting shade of this mango tree* could be of little interest to most people. I find refuge under its shade when I am there alone, secluded from the world and others, asking myself questions, or talking to myself. My talks are not always triggered by my questions.

There has to be an a priori reason that has been lost in the pleasure of finding refuge under the shade of this tree. What I should do is to totally let myself be taken by the feelings of being under it, to live it, and to make this experience more and more intense to the extent that I prove its existence.

To come under the shade of this mango tree with such deliberateness and to experience the fulfillment of solitude emphasize my need for communion. While I am physically alone proves that I understand the essentiality of to be *with*. It is interesting for me to think now how important, even indispensable, it is to be *with*. To be alone has represented for me throughout my lifetime a form of being *with*. I never avoid being with others as if I am afraid of company, as if I do not need others to feel fulfilled, or as if I feel awkward in the world. On the contrary, by isolating myself I get to know myself better while I recognize my limits, and the needs that involve me in a permanent search that would not be viable through

---

*An allusion to the Portuguese title of this volume. Cf. footnote page 8, in the foreword, as well as the preface, page 26.

isolation. I need the world as the world needs me. Isolation can only make sense when, instead of rejecting communion, it confirms it as a moment of its existence.

A negative isolation is to be found in those who timidly or methodically look to find some refuge in being alone. A negative isolation is characterized by those who selfishly require that everything revolves around them so as to meet their needs. This form of solitude is often required by those who only see themselves even when they are surrounded by a multitude of people. These individuals can only see themselves, their class, or their group due to their greed, which suffocates the rights of others. These types of people are characterized by the feeling that the more they have, the more they *want* to have—and it does not matter what means they use to achieve their ends. These are insensitive people who add arrogance and meanness to their insensitivity. These are the people who when they are in a good mood, call the popular classes "those people," and when they are in bad mood, refer to them as "trashy people."

Let me first make it clear that I refuse to accept a certain type of scientistic criticism that insinuates that I lack rigor in the way I deal with these issues or the overaffective language I use in this process. The passion with which I know, I speak, or I write does not, in any way, diminish the commitment with which I announce or denounce. I am a totality and not a dichotomy. I do not have a side of me that is schematic, meticulous, nationalist, and another side that is disarticulated or imprecise, which simply likes the world. I know with my entire body, with feelings, with passion, and also with reason.

I have been always engaged with many thoughts concerning the challenges that draw me to this or that issue or to the doubts that make me unquiet. These doubts take me to uncertainties, the only place where it is possible to work toward the necessary provisional certainties. It is not the case that it is impossible to be certain about some things. What is impossible is to be absolutely certain, as if the certainty of today were the same as that of yesterday and will continue to be the same as that of tomorrow.

In being methodical concerning the certainty of uncertainties does not deny the isolation of the cognitive possibility. The fundamental certainty is that I can know. *I know that I know.* In the same way, I also know that I do not know, which predisposes me to know the following: first, that I can know better what I know; second, that I can know what I do not know yet; third, that I can produce forms of knowledge that do not exist yet.

In being conscious that I can know socially and historically, I also know that what I know cannot be divorced from the historical continuity. Knowledge has historicity. It never is, it is always in the process of being. But this does not at all diminish, on the one hand, the fundamental certainty that I can know; on the other hand, it does not diminish the possibility of knowing with more methodological rigor that would enhance the level of the accuracy of the findings.

In order to know better what I already know implies, sometimes, to know what before was not possible to know. Thus, the important thing is to educate the curiosity through which knowledge is constituted as it grows and refines itself through the very exercise of knowing.

An education of answers does not at all help the curiosity that is indispensable in the cognitive process. On the contrary, this form of education emphasizes the mechanical memorization of contents. Only an education of question can trigger, motivate, and reinforce curiosity.

It is obvious that the mistake inherent in an education that forms only in giving answers does not reside in the answer itself but in the rupture between the answer and the question. The mistake lies in the fact that the answer is given independently from the question that triggers it. By the same token, an education of answer would be wrong if the answer is not perceived as part of the question. To question and to answer represent a constitutive path to curiosity.

It is necessary that we should always be expecting that a new knowledge will arise, transcending another that, in being new, would became old.

History, like us, is a process of being limited and conditioned by the knowledge that we produce. Nothing that we engender, live, think, and make explicit takes place outside of time and history. To be certain or to doubt would represent historical forms of being.

Life Support and the World

It would be unthinkable to have a world where the human experience took place outside of a continuity, that is, outside of history. The often-proclaimed "death of history" implies the death of women and men. We cannot survive the death of history: while it is constituted by us, it makes and remakes us. What occurs is the transcendence of a historical phase for another that does not eliminate the continuity of history in the depth of change itself.

It is impossible to change the world into something that is unappealingly immobile, within which nothing happens outside of what has been preestablished, to thereby create a world that is plane, horizontal, and timeless. The world, in order to be, must be in *the process of being*. A world that is plane, horizontal, and timeless could even be compatible with animal life but it remains incompatible with human existence. In this sense, the animals usually adapt to the life-support world, while human beings, in integrating themselves to their contexts so that they can intervene in them, transform the world. It is for this reason that we can tell stories about what happens in the life-support world, we talk about various forms of life that are formed in it. However, the history that is processed in the world is what is made by human beings.

If communication and intercommunication represent processes that speak to life about the support system, in the existential experience they acquire a special connotation. In this instance, both communication and intercommunication involve the comprehension of the world. The life-support world does not imply a language or the erect posture that permitted the liberation of the hands. The life-support becomes world and life becomes existence to the degree that there is an increasing solidarity between the mind and the hands. In other words, this change depends upon the proportion to which the human body becomes a conscient body that can capture, apprehend, and transform the world so it ceases being an empty space to be filled by contents.*

The process through which humans became erect, produced instruments, spoke, developed understanding, and began to communicate with one another represents tasks that involve solidarity and, simultaneously, imply cause and effect due to the presence of humans and their invention of the world as well as their domination over the life support. To be in the world necessarily implies being *with* the world and *with* others. For those beings who are simply in the life support, their activities in the life support represent a mere meddling; in the world with its social, historical, and cultural context, human beings interfere more than just merely meddle with the world.

In this sense, the shift from life support to world implies technical inventions and instruments that make the intervention in the world easier. Once these instruments are invented, men and women never stop the process of creating and reinventing new techniques with which they perfect their presence in the world. All operations in the world necessarily involve their comprehension, a knowledge about the process to operate in the world, an inventory about the findings but, above all, a vision with respect to the ends proposed in these operations. The creation intensifies to the degree that the

---

*See *The Cambridge Encyclopedia of Language.* Cambridge: Cambridge University Press, 1987.

rhythm of change is accelerated by developed techniques, which become more and more adequate to deal with these challenges.

The time period between significant changes in the world diminishes increasingly. In certain fields of science and the present technology, it takes a mere few months for the procedure to become obsolete. Sometimes, for reasons that are purely economic, these procedures have "a longer shelf life." This has to do with the resources spent in the development of a particular technological procedure or instruments that have not yet been operated, and, even though these procedures or instruments become obsolete, they continue to be considered efficient.

The ability to reflect, to evaluate, to program, to investigate, and to transform is unique to human beings in the world and with the world. Life becomes existence and life support becomes world when the conscience about the world, which also implies the conscience of the self, emerges and establishes a dialectical relationship with the world. The question between conscience/world that involves their mutual relations led Sartre to observe that "conscience and world take place at the same time." The relations between them are naturally dialectical, regardless of the school of thought and the philosophy that one studies. If one is a mechanist or an idealist, one cannot alter the dialectic conscience/world and subjectivity/objectivity. This does not mean that one mechanistic or idealistic practice is freed from its fundamental error. The plans of action that are based on the conception that conscience is the arbitrary maker of the world, and that defend the idea that before changing the world the moral conscience must be purified, will usually end up in a great failure. By the same token, projects that are based on a mechanistic vision in which the conscience is a mere reflex of the objective materiality cannot escape the punishment of history.

Many possible dreams end up not being viable due to the excess of certainty of their agents; and the capriciousness with which they pretended to mold history instead of making it with others would lead to a remaking of one another in the process. If history is not a superior entity that is above our heads and possesses us, it also cannot be reduced to an object to be manipulated.

By rejecting the dialectical tension between conscience/world, both idealists and mechanists, in their own way, become obstacles to connect intelligence of the world. This has been a theme that has always challenged me, one I have always attempted to address coherently with my democratic dream. Rarely do I find myself under the shadow of my mango tree without feeling unquiet and not thinking about this.

I am not a being in the life support but a being in the world, with the world, and with others; I am a being who makes things, knows and ignores, speaks, fears and takes risks, dreams and loves, becomes angry and is enchanted. I am a being who rejects the condition of being a mere object. I am a being who does not bow before the indisputable power accumulated by technology because, in knowing that it is a human production, I do not accept that it is, in and of itself, bad. I am a being who rejects a view of technology as a demon's deed designed to throw out God's work.*

It is not enough for me to ask: "What can one do? Technology necessarily engenders automatism, which leads to unemployment. The unemployed must change: they should seek leisure, a fundamental theme of postmodernity." No: I do not accept this form of fatalism.

The state cannot be so liberal as the neoliberals would like it to be. It behooves the progressive political parties to fight in favor of economic development and the limitation of the size of the state. The state should neither be an almighty entity nor a lackey that obeys the orders of those who live well. The projects of economic development cannot exclude men and women of history in the name of any fatalism.

---

*See Neil Postman. *Technology: The Surrender of Culture to Technology.* New York: Alfred A. Knopf, 1992.

My radical posture requires of me an absolute loyalty to all men and women. An economy that is incapable of developing programs according to human needs, and that coexists indifferently with the hunger of millions of people to whom everything is denied, does not deserve my respect as an educator. Above all, it does not deserve my respect as a human being. And it is not well to say, "Things are the way they are because they cannot be different." They cannot be different because if they were, they would be in conflict with the interests of the ruling class. This cannot, however, be the determining essence of the economic practice. I cannot become fatalistic in order to meet the interests of the ruling class. Neither can I invent a "scientific" explanation to cover up a lie **(see note 1, page 110)**.

The power of those in power always aims to decimate the powerless. But, alongside material power, there was always another force—ideology—which is also material and strengthens the power structure. Technological advances enhance with great efficiency the ideological support of material power.

One of the most important tasks for progressive intellectuals is to demystify postmodern discourses with respect to the inexorability of this situation. I vehemently reject such immobilization of history.

The affirmation that "Things are the way they are because they cannot be otherwise" is hatefully fatalistic since it decrees that happiness only belongs to those in power. The poor people, the disinherited, and those who have been excluded, were destined to die of cold no matter if they are from the South or the North of the world.

If the economic and political power of the ruling class denies the powerless the minimum space to survive, it is not because it should be that way. It is necessary that the weakness of the powerless is transformed into a force capable of announcing justice. For this to happen, a total denouncement of fatalism is necessary. We are transformative beings and not beings for accommodation.

We cannot reject the struggle for the exercise of our capacities and our rights to decide. In this way, I insist that *history is possibility and not determinism*. We are conditioned beings but not determined beings. It is impossible to understand history as possibility if we do not recognize human beings as beings who make free decisions. Without this form of exercise it is not worth speaking about ethics.

My First World

Because I am a being in the world and with the world, I have not a little piece of the life-support world, but I possess my more immediate and particular world: the street, the neighborhood, the city, the country, the yard of the house where I was born, where I learned to walk and to speak, where I had my first scares and fears. One day, when I was around five years old, I guessed that there was a relationship difficulty between my father and my mother. I did not have, neither *could* I have, the full awareness about the extent and depth of that situation. All of a sudden, I felt as if the ground was disappearing from under my feet. The insecurity weakened me. That night I could hardly sleep because of my fright. I dreamed that I was falling from a high precipice from which, with much effort, they miraculously saved me.

A sense of security slowly returned to the degree that, in needing it, I would search for it through the relationship between my mother and my father. When I woke up in the morning, I happily understood that my security depended on the way my parents spoke to each other and to me.

My first world was the yard in my house, with the mango trees, cashew trees with their branches kneeling down to the shaded ground, along with the breadfruit trees among others. These trees with their varied colors, smells, and fruits would attract various birds where they would take advantage of the space provided by the trees for them to sing (**see note 2, page 111**).

My childhood backyard has been unveiling itself to many other spaces—spaces that are not necessarily other yards. Spaces where this man of today sees the child of yesterday in himself and learns to see better what he had seen before. To see again what had already been seen before always implies seeing angles that were not perceived before. Thus, a posterior view of the world can be done in a more critical, less naive, and more rigorous way.

My childhood backyard constituted my immediate objectivity. It represented my other geographic point of reference where my other personal point of reference was represented by my parents, my brothers, my grandmother, my aunts and my nanny, a beloved black mother who became part of my family.

I was constituted by these different points of reference. I was realized as the *I* who made things, the thinking *I* and the speaking *I*.

When I thought that I had forgotten my childhood backyard and that I had little to do with it, one winter afternoon in Geneva, during my exile, it presented itself to me. During that afternoon while reading a letter I had received from Recife I—all of a sudden, like magic—recoiled into time and almost saw myself again as a child, in my backyard full of trees, learning to read with the help of my mother and father, writing phrases and words in the ground shaded by the mango trees. In that afternoon, it was as if I had discovered that the longing I was feeling for my homeland, had begun to be prepared by the *lived relationship* I had with my backyard.

The way Brazil exists for me could not have been possible without my backyard to which I later added streets, neighborhoods, and cities. The land that people love, talk about, and make reference to always has a backyard, a street, a street corner, a ground smell, a cutting cold, a suffocating heat, something for which we fight, we have specific needs, and we have a language that is spoken with different intonations. This is a homeland for which we sometimes lose sleep, a distant land that causes us some unquietness that has to do with one's backyard, one's street corners, and one's dreams. In certain moments, our love for our backyard is extended to other places and, it ends up fixing itself in a large place where we make our home, we plant our seed, our city.

Before I could become a citizen of the world I was and am first a citizen of Recife. The more rooted I am in my location, the more I extend myself to other places so as to become a citizen of the world. No one becomes local from a universal location. The existential road is the reverse. I am citizen of Recife. I am first from Recife, from Pernanbuco, and a North-eastern. Afterward, I became a Brazilian, a Latin American, and a world citizen. It is for this reason that my longing was not exclusively for Recife. It included the longing for my backyard. However, my longing for Brazil, that also included my longing for Recife that made it authentic, was not limited to Recife only. My longings were also not limited to the more particular places such as certain street corners, or plazas such as the Casa Plaza.

Because I was longing for Brazil, I was also longing for Recife, Rio, Natal, Porto Alegre, Manaus, Fortaleza, Coritiba, João Pessoa, and Gioania. I missed Brazil in its totality, in its unity within diversity, which I express when I say without arrogance: "I am Brazilian, full of confidence, with an identity, with the hope that in our struggle we will remake ourselves by making a society that is less unjust."

When I say, "I am Brazilian," I feel something more than when I say, "I am from Recife." But I also know I could feel so intensely Brazilian without first recognizing Recife, my original signpost where my Brazilianism is generated. For this reason, let me express the obvious that my homeland is not the only geographic point I retain with much clarity in my memory, and that I can reproduce with my eyes closed. My homeland is, above all, a space in time that involves geography, history, culture. My homeland is also pain, hunger, misery. It is also the hope of millions who remain hungry for social justice.

My homeland is the dramatic coexistence of different times that come together in the same geographical space—backwardness, misery, poverty, hunger, traditionalism, magical conscience, authoritarianism, democracy, modernity, and postmodernity. The Brazilian professor who discusses education and postmodernity in the university is the same person who must live with the cruel reality of millions of men and women who are dying of hunger.

My homeland is filled with the beauty of waterfalls, rivers, beaches, flowers, animals, and birds. When I think about my homeland, I begin to see how much more we must travel to struggle so as to transcend the pervasive structures of exploitation. That is why when I was forced to be away from my homeland, my nostalgia was never reduced to a sad cry or a desperate complaint. I used to think of it, as I continue to do so, as a contradictory historical space that requires of me—wherever I am presented with a decision to make—to take a position, to rupture, to opt (see note 3, page 111).

In being in favor of something or someone, I am necessarily against someone. Thus, it is necessary to ask: "With whom am I? Against what and whom am I?" To think about my homeland when asking these questions and without answering them, would lead me to pure idealizations that are removed from reality. The lack of clarity with respect to the problems involved in these inquiries and the lack of interest toward these problems make us complicit with the violent oppressors and with the (dis)order that benefits them.

To serve the dominant order is what many intellectuals of today who were progressive yesterday are doing when they reject all educational practices that unveil the dominant ideology while reducing education to a mere transference of contents that are considered "sufficient" to guarantee a happy life. They consider a happy life that in which one lives by adapting to a world without anger, without protests, and without dreams of transformation. What is ironic in this enthusiastic adherence to the present pragmatism by old progressive militants is that, in embracing what appears to them to be new, they are reincarnating old formulas that are necessary to preserve the power of the dominant class.

And they do this with the appearance of considering themselves up-to-date and able to transcend "old ideologies." They speak of the great need of professionalizing pedagogical programs even if they are empty of any possibility to understand society critically. This statement is made under the progressive rubric! However, this statement is just as conservative as an educational practice is falsely progressive when it rejects the technical preparation of students so as to focus only on the political dimension of education. The technical mastery is just as important for students as the political understanding is for a citizen. It is not possible to separate them.

A good carpenter who does not fight to expand his or her political space, or who does not socially struggle to make his or her trade better and, by the same token, a good engineer who avoids the struggle for the rights of a citizen, ends up working against the professional efficacy of their trade.

As women and men, we continue to be what Aristotle said so well. We are political animals. We continue to be that into which we have turned: political animals.

For all of this, my homeland holds my dream of freedom—a freedom that I cannot impose on others but for which I have always fought. To think of my homeland is to nurture my dream. It is a form of fighting for it. I never thought of my homeland in a myopic manner: it is not superior nor inferior to other lands. Our homeland is constituted by its geography, its ecology, and its biology; it is also what we, as women and men, make of it. Our homeland depends on how we organize its production, its history, its education, its culture, its food and the taste we develop for it. Our homeland involves a struggle for different dreams that are sometimes in antagonistic relationship due to the existence of the social classes that inform it. Our homeland is, in the end, an abstraction.

Hope

When I think about my homeland, I am reminded both of the smugness of the rich, their anger toward the poor, and of the poor's lack of hope, forged in their long-lived experience with exploitation or in the hope gestated in their struggle for justice.

"I am a countryman, sir. I have no tomorrow that is any different from today, that is any different from yesterday," a man, still young, from the Forest Zone in Pernambuco once told me. If, however, that man has participated in the struggle of the Rural Leagues, this experience might have helped to change his understanding of the facts and his "reading of the world." His fatalism might have turned into a possible dream. It might have become the utopia of liberation, which he will have begun to understand as a social process against the force that crushes him. At this point, he absolutely knows he has a future. Not one certain future for exploited countrymen and another, as he used to think, equally unappealable for the dominant. His political practice will have taught him that his future lies in the transformation of a perverse today where he and his fellow countrymen and countrywomen are *quasi persons*. He thus understands the problematization of the future rather than its inexorability. Such a future will not come if we do not speak about it at the same time that we make it. The future is not a donation: it exists as a necessity of history and implies its continuity. History has not died, nor has it metamorphosed into a make-believe mirage (**see note 4, page 115**).

The Forest Zone countryman's talk, under the burden of *existential weariness*, explained a fatalistic view of his own presence in the world. Such a view is as fatalistic as that of the mechanistic, antidialectic intellectual, for whom the future is inexorable. It is as fatalistic as the intellectual of postmodernity, who while describing the obstacles the new time poses to liberation, proclaims them insurmountable. For these fatalistic intellectuals, there is no longer *viable novelty*. (Paulo Freire, *Pedagogy of Hope*. New York: Continuum, 1994).

Such profoundly resigned attitude characterizes the comprehension modes and the practices of yesterday's progressives, the pragmatic of today, in the present world. Leftists who used to criticize me as a "bourgeois idealist" now, pragmatic and neoliberal, point me out as just another dreamer. "The compulsive dreamer speaks of change when there is nothing left to change," they say, while reassured rather than disillusioned.

Recently in Bavaria, a German educator friend mentioned having heard from a "leftist" activist: "Paulo Freire no longer makes any sense. The education needed today has nothing to do with dreams, utopias, conscientiousness; but rather with the technical, scientific, and professional development of learners." "Development," here is understood as training. This is exactly what has always interested the dominant classes: the depoliticization of education. In reality, education requires technical, scientific, and professional development as much as it does dreams and utopia.

I reject the notion that nothing can be done about the consequences of economic globalization and refuse to bow my head gently because nothing can be done against the unavoidable. Accepting the inexorability of what takes place is an excellent contribution to the dominant forces in their unequal fight against the "condemned of the earth."

One of the fundamental differences between me and such fatalistic intellectuals—sociologists, economists, philosophers, or educators, it does not matter—lies in my never accepting, yesterday or today, that educational practice should be restricted to a "reading of the word," a "reading of text," but rather believing that it should also include a "reading of context," a "reading of the world." Above all, my difference lies in my critical, in-no-way-naive optimism and in the hope that encourages me, and that does not exist for the fatalistic.

This is a hope that originates in the very nature of human beings. Being inconclusive and conscious of their inconclusion—or as François Jacob puts it, "programmed to learn"—human beings could not *be* without the impulse of hope.

Hope is an ontological requirement for human beings. However, to the extent that men and women have become beings who relate to the world and to others, their historical nature is conditioned to the possibility of becoming concrete, or not.

Hope of liberation does not mean liberation already. It is necessary to fight for it, within historically favorable conditions. If they do not exist, we must hopefully labor to create them. Liberation is a possibility, not fate nor destiny nor burden. In this context, one can realize the importance of education for decision, for rupture, for choice, for ethics at last.

For this reason, the more subjected and less able to dream of freedom that they are, the less able will concrete human beings be to face their challenges. The more of a sombering present there is, one in which the future is drowned, the less hope there will be for the oppressed and the more peace there will be for the oppressors. Thus, education in the service of domination cannot cause critical and dialectic thinking; rather it stimulates naive thinking about the world.

While thinking about my homeland, I cannot ignore these varieties of thinking. Not only do they express concrete situations that condition them, but also they reorient our actions upon reality. Obviously, the countryman's fatalistic understanding—"we have no tomorrow"—makes him not viable. His engagement in some sort of fight would imply his overcoming that understanding.

Although a progressive educator, I must not reduce my instructional practice to the sole teaching of technique or content, leaving untouched the exercise of a critical understanding of reality. In speaking about hunger, I must not be satisfied with defining it as "urgent need for food, big appetite, lack of nourishment, deprivation from, or scarcity of food." The critical intelligence of something implies the apprehension of its reason for being. Stopping at the description of the object or twisting its reasons for being are mind-narrowing processes. My comprehension of hunger is not *dictionary:* once recognizing the meaning of the word, I must recognize the reasons for the phenomenon. If I cannot be indifferent to the pain of those who go hungry, I cannot suggest to them either that their situation is the result of God's will. That is a lie.

Once, in a TV report about landless rural workers in the interior of São Paulo, the reporter asked a country adolescent, "Do you usually dream?" "No, I only have nightmares," he replied. What was fundamental in his answer was his fatalist, immobilist understanding. The bitterness of that adolescent's existence was so profound that his presence in the world had become a *nightmare,* an experience in which it was impossible *to dream.* "I only have nightmares," he repeated, as if to insist that the reporter never forget that fact. He could not see a future for himself.

Without a vision for tomorrow, hope is impossible. The past does not generate hope, except for the time when one is reminded of rebellious, daring moments of fight. The past, understood as immobilization of what was, generates longing, even worse, *nostalgia,* which nullifies tomorrow. Almost always, concrete situations of oppression reduce the oppressed's historical time to an everlasting present of hopelessness and resignation. The oppressed grandchild repeats the suffering of their grandparent. This is what happens to the oppressed majorities in the Northeast of this country, existentially tired and historically anesthetized that they are **(see note 5, page 115)**.

Tired and anesthetized, in need of everything, they are easy prey for aid-and-assistance policies that further immerse them in a mind-narrowing daily existence. Such must not be the politics of a progressive government, which in *assisting* the needy, those precluded from being, must never *assistancialize* them.

One of the main differences between assistance policies and those that assist without "assistencializing" is that the former insist on the suggestion that the great big problem with the oppressed lies in deficiencies of nature; the latter, on the other hand, underscores the importance of the social, the economic, and the political: in sum, power.

After a few years, I hope that teenage boy may have realized that, in such a dehumanizing society, our dream materialized into political struggle, so as to overcome the nightmare to which the dominant class reduces the existence of the poor. I hope he has come to understand that transformation is not brought about with the approval of landlords or of other people, but rather with his own decided opposition. It is necessary for us to defeat these lords—whose speeches promise what they know they cannot deliver—by voting them down. Thus, it is urgent that the disowned unite and that we all fight in favor of liberation, transforming this offensive world into a more *people-oriented* one, from both a political and an ethical standpoint, I should add.

When I think about my homeland, I think, above all, about the possible dream, if not at all an easy one, of democratically inventing our society. Speaking of that, I must return to my criticism of the pragmatic neoliberal position, according to which an effective educational practice today must be centered in technical training or in the deposit of content into the learners. In that case, the selection and organization of the content to be taught in the schools would be up to specialists.

The neoliberal point of view reinforces a pseudoneutrality of the educational practice, reducing it to the transfer of informational content to the learners, who are not required to apprehend it in order to learn it. Such "neutrality" serves as the foundation for reducing the education of a plumber to training in the techniques and procedures involved in wrench mastering. Every educational practice that goes beyond that—which avoids the *reading of the word/reading of the world, reading of text/reading of context* dichotomy—will not gain pedagogical endorsement and shall become mere *ideology.* Worse yet, it will be considered inappropriate for the present moment, one without social classes, without conflict, without dreams, without utopia.

Such ideological separation between text and context, between an object and its reason for being, implies regrettable error; it involves taking away the learners' *epistemological curiosity.* For this reason, as it accepts the notion of more education for the working class, the dominant class bumps into its limits. Even the most progressive and democratic businessperson will always be limited by the interests of his or her social class. If the businessperson overcomes this limit and accepts a progressive variety of education, he or she will wind up working against himself or herself. It is possible that some businessperson may venture into such "conversion"; that is not the case with the class as a whole. History has yet to record any case of class suicide.

I would like to call attention to an implication present in a veiled manner within neoliberal discourse. When they speak about the death of history, of ideologies, of utopia, and about the disappearance of social classes, they make me certain that they defend a posterior sort of fatalism. It is as if they regret not having stated the *domestication* of the future sooner. The mechanists of Marxist origin *deproblematized* the future and reduced it to a premade, preknown time; those who now defend the end of history welcome the "new time," the time of "definitive victory" for capitalism, as a future that was late in coming, but that is finally here. They wipe out sixty years of human achievement with a sponge, considering it an error of history finally corrected. According to such discourse, having reached the levels it has, as it created the social classes of modern society, the capitalist system would have a greater purpose than the one Marx attributed to the working class: being the undertaker of the dominant class. As it constituted itself, the capitalist system was doomed to end with history itself.

We had a long conversation about that in Prague—Nita (my wife) and myself with Karel Kosik, the notable Czech philosopher, author of *Dialectics of the Concrete*. We spoke about the dogmatism of authoritarian socialism, about its inflexibility, the deproblematization of the future, and thus about its domestication, the future as a time already known, as a given fact rather than a time in progress. We spoke about the senselessness and rudeness of bureaucrats, about their sectarian blindness, their attraction to immobility, to death.

We reminisced about a letter Kosik wrote Sartre in the seventies, in which he denounced the invasion of his house by police, who took his philosophic manuscripts and promised to return them as soon as they had read them. I remembered Kosik's humor in telling Sartre about "being certain of having lost the manuscripts" if the police's reading them was to be a condition for their return.

I remembered Sartre's letter published in *Le Mond* in reply to Kosik. It was critical, energetic, and lucid. One of the important records in this century of intelligence against stupidity, of freedom against despotism, of hope against fatalism.

It is not true that capitalism is the radiant future we have already come to. Reality is not only blue or only green: it is multicolored, a rainbow. I am writing this page in a hotel in Bavaria, in Munich, in an afternoon when the thermometer, indicating thirty-eight degrees fahrenheit, would intimidate any Recifean.

German educators, some old friends from the seventies, report on how frequent the complaints and wounded hopes of men and women "on the other side" became and on how, weary from the limitation of their freedom, they dreamed of the "opening" of the capitalist world. They dreamed of an ocean of roses that they did not find.

Some of the reports I have heard support my initial reaction to the disintegration of authoritarian socialism. To me, this disintegration always seemed to imply some sort of *ode to freedom*, without that representing any negation of its fundamental reasons, material ones and ones of an economic nature, added to those of a technological order.

None of the reports from those who have been disenchanted with the capitalist world has revealed nostalgia over the authoritarian, bureaucratic, and asphyxiating experience of "realist socialism." And, since I do not believe Stalinist authoritarianism is part of the nature of socialism, I have no reason to admit that a truly democratic socialism is an impossible proposition.

I refuse to accept that the presence of authoritarianism within socialism is due to some ontological incompatibility between human beings and the essence of socialism. That would be the same as saying: "So averse is human nature to the fundamental virtues of socialism that only under coercion would it be possible to make it work." That which human ontology rejects, on the contrary, is authoritarianism, regardless of what attributes it may receive.

I have met educators from the former East Germany who tell me, not just to be polite, that it is finally possible for them to read my work and that they regret having experienced a time when, in the least, such reading would have been made difficult.

Let us return once again to my homeland.

I could never think of it in romantic terms exclusively. If it is impossible for me to kill all that is romantic in my relationship with my homeland, I must not reduce my comprehension of it to my desire to transform it. When I underscore its beauty, I must also emphasize the popular masses' interdiction from enjoying such beauty.

A "no-man's land," it is surrendered to the generations as they come; whether "finished" or "lost," it is always in process of being. An important factor, if not the only one, in this process is the conflict of interests between the dominant and the dominated. It is from the starting point of the concrete reality new generations come to face, that it becomes possible to articulate dreams of re-creating society.

As I speak about my homeland, I describe an ideal shared in communion with a countless number of Brazilians: the realization of a land where loving may be less difficult and where the popular classes may have a voice, rather than becoming frightened shadows before the arrogance of the powerful.

When I speak about my homeland, I do not refer only to the beauties of Rio, of the Guanabara Bay, of Christ the Redeemer, of the waterfalls Brazil is so rich in; I don't only speak of the beaches in the Northeast, their warm waters, of the Pantanal and the Amazon, of Villa Lobos's Studies, of Carlos Gomes's music, of Aleijadinho's art, of samba and its Schools, of Carnaval, popular music, soccer, the country's art, its science, and Brasilia. I also refer to the hunger of millions, to degrading destitution, to murdered children, to established disorder, to swindling, to the everpresent authoritarianism, and to multiplying violence. I refer to the class *war* raging throughout the country, perhaps, that is too hard-hitting in Rio. It is a class war that hides and makes confusing a frustrated *class struggle.* All that also makes up my homeland. And I cannot cross my arms, indifferent, before any of this. The homeland of my dreams is my homeland rid of all such horrors.

No society can rid itself of these horrors by decree, or just because some of its fundamental, active subjects, the dominant, happen to bestow, in a gesture of love, a whole new way of life upon the "condemned of the land." Overcoming these horrors implies a political decision, popular mobilization, organization, political intervention, and lucid, hopeful, coherent, tolerant leadership.

While a virtue, *tolerance* does not grow on trees, neither is it a concept that can be learned through mechanical transference, from a speaking, active subject who deposits it into subdued patients. The learning of tolerance takes place through testimony. Above all, it implies that, while fighting for my dream, I must not become passionately closed within myself. It is necessary that I open myself to knowledge and refuse to isolate myself within the circle of my own truth or reject all that is different from it or from me. Tolerance is the open, postmodernly progressive way for me, while living with the different, to learn from it and better fight the antagonistic. Unprotected by *coherence*, however, tolerance runs the risk of losing itself. Coherence between what we say and do sets limits to tolerance and keeps it from derailing into *connivance*. For example, in coexisting with neoliberals, I may discuss our positions. I cannot, however, enter agreements from which concessions would result that might deteriorate my strategic dream. In that case, I would be not tolerant but rather conniving with the pollution of my dream.

The Limit of the Right

If, however, in a given political context I come to be considered a *lesser evil* by the neoliberal, I cannot keep them from voting for me. They are free to do that. What is up to me in this case is to refuse to accept that their tacit vote would be turned into a favor, an element of bargaining. Their voting for me does not make them into my journey companions, nor should it put me in a position to have to promote them politically.

There is another context, a dramatic one, where an activist of truly progressive tradition happily accepts being the *right's limit*. To settle into such a position is to run an excessively high risk of becoming right.

It is easy to fall into such contradiction, jeopardizing much of the dream in shady alliances; it is hard to secure coherent agreements. What is most common is for there to be fighting between the alike and rupture between the different, as if they were antagonistic. I have no doubt that unity within diversity imposes itself to the lefts (plural) as a means to defeating the right (singular) and, thus, democratizing society.

Latin Americans of the left incur an error that I find to be dangerous—and that tends to intensify—as they move backward, believing to be moving forward, in search of the elusive *center*. It is almost always the case that a less perverse right or one self-proclaimed *center* intends to make its reactionarism more suave. It always remains right, though.

In light of the collapse of the socialist world, perplexed leftist activists have been turning *pragmatic* and *centrist*. That alone is no major concern. We all have the right to change, to think and act today in a different way from yesterday. Besides, no one who goes through such change has any reason to hide it. But I am precluded from understanding by reality; how one could justify the change by saying that social classes have disappeared, thus altering the essence of conflicts by removing their social-class-generated antagonistic character. I cannot understand how one would *adopt* the center as the left's new address, how one could move to the center as if that were the only place progressive forces could aspire to today.

I do not accept this form of fatalism also. It is as if, in order to be left, one necessarily has to go through the center; in order to be progressive one needs to go through a conservative stage.

It is one thing to realize that the popular classes have become uninterested in ideological discourses that drift into rambling babble; it is quite another to say that ideologies have died. The popular majority's lack of interest in ideological analyses is not enough to kill ideologies. This very lack of interests is an ideological expression: ideologies can only be ideologically killed.

While converting to democracy and becoming no longer parties of *ranks*, leftist parties must become truly pedagogical instruments. They must respond to the demands of their time and become capable of inventing communication channels to the expropriated and to those adhering to them.

A democratic style of doing politics, especially in societies with strong authoritarian traditions, requires concretely acquiring a taste for freedom, for commitment to the rights of others, and for tolerance as a life-guiding rule. The leftist parties that authenticate themselves through the effort of unveiling truths must not renounce their fundamental task, which is critical-educational.

Instead of converting myself to the center and occasionally coming to power, as a progressive, I would rather embrace democratic pedagogy and, not knowing when, attain power along with the popular classes in order to reinvent it.

The lefts' sectarianism and dogmatism were always most unbearable and made them almost "religious," as they construed themselves into holders of the truth, with their excessive certainty, their authoritarianism, and their mechanistic understanding of history and of conscience. The results of all that were the deproblematization of the future and the decrease of conscience, reflections of the external reality.

This deproblematization of the future and mechanization of science/world relations seriously weakened, and even negated, the ethical nature of world transformation, since opting for other paths was not a possibility. The future was inexorable rather than problematic. Thus, there ensued a lack of concern for pedagogical work, which was put on hold awaiting infrastructural transformation. The final result was the rejection of dreaming, of utopia, very much like today's *pragmatics.*

"Is there a way out for Brazil?" This question is constantly posed to me, and once in a while I bring it with me under my metaphorical tree. My answer is *yes.* Except that there is a way out only to the extent that we are determined to forge it. There is no way out that will become visible by chance.

Societies do not constitute themselves due to the fact that they are this or that; it is not their destiny to be not serious or to be examples of honor. Societies are *not;* they are in the process of being what we make of them in history, as a possibility. Thus, we have an ethical responsibility.

If history were *a time of determinism,* one where every *present* necessarily were the future expected yesterday, and every tomorrow were something already known, there would be no room for opting, for rupture. Social struggle would be reduced to either delaying the inexorable future or helping it *arrive.* One efficient way to delay it is to reproduce the present with cosmetic changes that pass as requirements of "modernity."

The struggle would be between those who, satisfied with today, would make an effort to delay the future as much as possible, to put up obstacles against any substantive change, and those who, exploited today, aspire to a new reality.

Tactic, the jargon of the satisfied, includes true aspects of society's dynamic present, except that they mold those to their ideology. Basing themselves on a real concern, for example, the discussion around the size of government, they advocate its almost complete absence or a role for it of mere management for the powerful.

Thus, we see the greediness with which they defend the privatization of every public company that turns a profit; we see the aggressiveness with which they attack anyone who, while defending a new understanding of the tasks and limits of government, rebels against its confinement to the role of defending the interests of the rich. Democratic fighters are referred to as "old," charged with not having historic *feeling,* and called *antiquity defenders,* having nothing to do with neoliberal modernity. At the same time, the "modern" files away at rigorous agrarian reform, without which any serious transformation is shot dead. Not one modern capitalist society has failed to conduct its agrarian reform, indispensable to the creation and maintenance of a domestic market. That is why among those democracies, agrarian reform is no longer discussed, and not because this process is "ancient" or a "violation of private property."

Once in Africa, I was told that a convenient way to capture monkeys was to prepare as natural a site as possible where a bag of corn was to be placed, tied to a tree trunk. The top portion of the bag was to contain a round wire frame allowing the monkeys to get into and out of the bag easily with their hands, provided that no corn was being held. The monkeys imprison themselves, for once they grab any corn, they never let go.

Within an understanding of history as possibility, tomorrow is problematic. In order for it to come, it is necessary that we build it through transforming today. Different tomorrows are possible. The struggle is no longer reduced to either delaying what is to come or ensuring its arrival; it is necessary to reinvent the future. Education is indispensable for this reinvention. By accepting ourselves as active subjects and objects of history, we become beings who make division. It makes us ethical beings.

Here lies one of the mistakes of some postmodernists who, while recognizing the requirement for fast decisions, brought about by technological advances, in this new historic time, state the contemporariness of a critical pedagogy, which assigns strategic value to the education of women and men capable of realizing, comparing, opting, and naturally, acting. Indeed, the need to make decisions quickly is an important act in societies where information and communication become accelerated. The fundamental problem for the centers of power lies in how to produce so specialized a variety of criticalness that decisions will be produced in line with the truth of the strong—the oppressors—and will always negate the truth of the weak.

Neoliberals and Progressives

From the point of view of neoliberal power and ideology, critical pedagogy is solely concerned with how promptly problems of a technical nature and bureaucratic difficulties can be overcome. Still in this view, social and political-ideological issues do not integrate the spectrum of concerns akin to educational practice, which is essentially *neutral*. This characteristic must be maintained in the *training* and *education* of young workers, in need of technical knowledge that can qualify them for the world of production.

We both, neoliberals and progressives, agree with the current demands of technology. However, we drastically diverge in our pedagogical-political response to them.

For we progressives, there is no thinking about technical education in itself, one that does not inquire in favor of what or whom, or against what it operates. From a pragmatist point of view, since there is no right or left any longer, it is important to make people more competent to deal with the difficulties with which they are faced.

One of the fundamental differences between a pragmatic and a progressive is that what is *strategic* to the pragmatic may, under special circumstances, be considered *tactical* to the progressive, whereas what is strategic to the latter is always rejected by the former.

In spite of the differences between the nineteenth century and the present time—which require a refinement of analytical methods, technical reformulations, production of new knowledge—the domination of the majority by the few has not disappeared. I would like to emphasize the uncomfortable situation of Third World intellectuals. Contemporary of their First World colleagues, they discuss postmodernity with them while living with the uncontrolled exploitation characteristic of a dependent, perverse, and outdated capitalism.

Brazilian intellectuals who state that today's fundamental topic is no longer *work* but *leisure*, are dealing with a reality in which 33 million out of 150 million Brazilians die of starvation.

Today's permanent and increasingly accelerated revolution of technology, the main bastion of capitalism against socialism, alters socioeconomic reality and requires a new comprehension of the facts upon which new political action must be founded. Today it is no longer possible to use, in the more modern areas of the Third World, political tactics that were efficient in the middle of the century.

I feel serious work, meticulous research, and critical reflection about dominant power, which is gaining increasing dimensions, have never been as needed as they are today. The activity of progressive intellectuals must never equate that of people who, recognizing the strength of obstacles, consider them to be insurmountable. That would be a fatalistic position, alien to the task of the progressive. Understanding obstacles as challenges, the progressive must search for appropriate answers.

In light of the existing dominion over information, of the ease with which it is managed by and communicated to the network of power, it is not difficult to imagine the difficulties faced by those operating at the extremities of the circuit. How limited is the power of those, for example, working in the soybean fields of Brazil, who can hardly imagine that the possibilities of their production are known with long notice at the Chicago stock exchange.

> One of the main political implications of the possession and utilization of technology associated with remote monitoring and geographic information systems is the ability to make predictions regarding the environment. Environment here is understood as the physical, historical, and social-economic substratum created from the dialectic confrontation between nature and man.

> The above-mentioned technologies make it possible to carry out, with cartographic precision, the tasks of defining location and area of occurrence, classifying, evaluating, and predicting environmental phenomena, generating essential information to support political-economic decisions concerning the use of environmental resources.

> Such technological support may be directed toward the early assessment, for example, of expected agricultural crops as

good or bad; in this case, fabulous profit may be generated
in the commodity markets based on early information.
(Letter from Professor Jorge Xavier da Silva,
Federal University of Rio de Janeiro, to the author, 1994)

Also, what to say about the ease with which production can
be transferred from one area of the world to another, making
workers more vulnerable? Their vulnerability decreases their
disposition to fight. It is possible that, with the growing globalization of the economy, strikes may lose efficacy in certain
sectors of production.

All that and much more makes the domination power of
the few over the many more robust and makes the struggle of
the latter extremely difficult. Recognizing, however, the tragic
nature of our times does not mean surrender. The struggle of
men and women may find obstacles; victory may be delayed,
but never suppressed.

In place of immobilist fatalism, I propose critical optimism,
one that may engage us in the struggle toward knowing, knowing on a par with our times and at the service of the exploited.

As I speak with such hope about the possibility of changing
the world, I do not intend to sound like a lyrical, naive educator. Even though I may speak in this fashion, I do not ignore
how much more difficult it is becoming to focus on the needs
of the oppressed, of those kept from being. I recognize the
obstacles the "new order" represents to the most fragile *pieces*
of the world, such as its intellectuals, obstacles that push them
into fatalist positions before the concentration of power.

I recognize reality. I recognize the obstacles, but I refuse to
resign in silence or to be reduced to a soft, ashamed, skeptical
echo of the dominant discourse. The quixotic position of Berenger has always excited me. From the beginning, he was
always in opposition to his fellows, who one by one, became
rhinoceroses in spite of his plea:

Ma Carabine, Ma Carabine!
Contre tout le monde, je me

defendrait! Je suis le dernier
homme, je le resterai jusqu'au
bout! Je ne capitule pas!
(Eugène Ionesco, Rhinoceros,
Paris: Éditions Gallimard, 1959, p. 246)

I like being a person precisely because of my ethical and political responsibility before the world and other people. I cannot be if others are not; above all, I cannot be if I forbid others from being. I am a human being. I am a man and not a rhinoceros as Berenger shouts.

Democratic Administration

When today Lula* states that an agreement over the much-needed agrarian reform would be preferable to an insufficiently discussed law, that does not mean this struggle has become less urgent to him.

Lula knows—today much better than the average of the left-ist leadership of yesterday and than the representatives of a certain outdated left of today—that there is a language of historic possibility, neither falling short of nor going beyond limits.

Contrary to what the irresponsible may think, the language of those who are immersed in our contradictory reality moved by the dream of making it less perverse is the language of possibility. It is the restrained language of those fighting for their utopia, those impatiently patient. It is not the discourse of those who boast a power they do not have, threatening the whole world. It is the talk of those who are certain of the ethic

*Luiz Ignacio Lula da Silva, or *Lula* as he is better known, is a historic political figure in Brazil. One of the founders of PT, the Workers' Party, he comes from a working-class background. Through his active union leadership in São Paulo, he became a symbol of progressive politics and ran for president against Fernando Collor de Melo, losing by a tight margin, in 1989.

rigor of their fight and their dream against the perversity of a society of inequality such as ours, those who do all in their power to mobilize and organize the popular classes and other segments of society toward the democratic institution of a fair government. Such a government would represent a party that accepted the alternate nature of democracy and, as a result, was continually exposed to popular judgment. Such position demands a fundamental sort of learning: that of *humility*, which requires that one respect adverse judgment from the people and, at the same time, that one not be able to doubt the utopia of democracy.

In reality, if we do all we can to make school more democratic, quantitatively and qualitatively, we will be confident in our progressive choice, not caring whether we win the next election or not. The fact that we have not gotten approved our proposed model for the general treatment of public property, health, education, and culture does not invalidate the democratic dream. I cannot allow my understanding of the world to become elitist just because I have lost a democratic election; what I do need is to continue in my struggle for the improvement and democratization of the institutions within society. I must not simply blame the people either, making the population responsible for not knowing how to vote or for being ungrateful. I must identify the presence of the ruling ideology, the strength of this ideology, and the democratic inexperience that is deeply rooted in our traditions. For example, after Senator Eduardo Suplicy's defeat in the race for mayor of São Paulo, after Luiza Erundina's administration, we could not accept a single one of the following propositions:

- our political dream of a less perverse society no longer makes sense
- our effort within Luiza Erundina's government was a mistake
- the people cannot vote because they did not choose the PT candidate.

None of these statements is correct. I must say that the effort we made at the City Department of Education, within the Erundina administration (1989–92), was politically serious, democratic, and scientifically founded. We have no reason to regret the administrative reform we implemented at the department toward decentralizing decisions. Without it, it would have been less easy to encourage democratic modes of behavior.

Administrative structures at the service of centralized power do not foster democratic behavior. One of the roles of democratic leaderships is precisely overcoming authoritarian systems and creating the conditions for decision making of a dialogic nature. Brazilian *centralism*, which Aluísio Teixeira fought so much against, was an expression of our authoritarian tradition and fed into it **(see note 6, page 118)**.

Also, we have no reason to regret the work we did in the area of continual professional development for teachers. This work was based on critical reflection over educational practice and counted on important contributions from professors of the Pontifical Catholic University of São Paulo (PUC), of the State University of Campinas (UNICAMP), and of the University of São Paulo (USP). In particular, it counted on the contribution of Professor Madalena Weffort, one of the most respected specialists in this area.

The urgently needed improvement in the quality of our education is linked to increased respect for educators, through significant improvement of their salaries, through *continual development*, and through reform of teaching preparation programs. All this implies the participation of Brazilian universities, since this development task is not restricted to schools of education. That is what we did, my team and I, when I was Secretary of Education for the city of São Paulo. I spoke at length with the presidents of PUC, UNICAMP, and USP, and then we signed cooperation agreements. We counted on the support of linguists, mathematicians, computer specialists, philosophers, specialists in curriculum theory, and sex educators. In this particular field, I would like to emphasize the excellent work of Marta Suplicy and of the Group for Work and Research in Sexual Orientation (GTPOS). It was no coincidence that during the Erundina administration we were able to surpass the school-success rates of an entire decade.

One of the crucial problems with Brazilian education—mistakenly termed *school evasion*, in reality *school expulsion*—is political-ideological. Its solution is linked to the professional development of educators and implies a political and ideological comprehension of language on their part, one that allows them to realize the class nature of speech. The alarming rate of school failure in literacy grades is connected to the lack of scientific preparation on the part of educators, and it also has to do with an elitist ideology that discriminates against popular boys and girls. In part, this explains the existing contempt for the learners' cultural identity, the disrespect for popular syntax, and the almost complete disregard for the learners' baggage of experiential knowledge.

During that period at the Department of Education, we observed gradual improvement in performance on the part of students, as the pedagogy of questioning started to gain ground against the pedagogy of answers, and as issues around the body were addressed in the Sexual Orientation Program. A more critical knowledge about the *conscious body* and experience in dealing with questions stimulated the development of epistemological curiosity.

We have no reason to regret the democratic fashion in which we administered the department, through committees, the base of which was the School Council. The council played more than a consulting role, in effect having decision-making power. We have no reason to regret our having insisted that public schools become popular and democratic—in other words, less authoritarian and elitist. We have no reason to regret having worked a reorientation of the curriculum in process. We have no reason to regret the evaluation and development seminars for technical personnel within the centers for Educational Action, held with vigilantes and other workers in the public schools. We have nothing to apologize for concerning the popular rallies, where we discussed our proposals and actions.

How could we blame ourselves for having organized evaluation seminars involving schools of different areas and two conferences on local education, both of which counted on extraordinary participation of the entire school system (see note 7, page 119)?

Finally, how could we apologize for the First Conference on Adult Literacy Learners? It was a forum where the learners had voice and not one where they were just talked about (see note 8, page 122).

Without humility, it would be difficult to carry out such a program. Thus, the learning of another virtue becomes a requirement: *perseverance*, the tenacity with which we must fight for our dream. We should not give up at the first confrontations, but with them, learn how to make fewer mistakes. In the life span of a person, five, ten, twenty years represent something, sometimes a lot, but that is not the case in the history of a nation.

If we are progressive, if we have more experience as opposition than as government, we must be reminded that, in such a historic moment as ours, it is easier to win elections than it is to govern. As we strongly react against the defamatory accusations leveled against us, may we not allow ourselves to adopt the same untruthful language used against us?

We must also observe, with ethical rigor, our right and our duty to speak about how we intend to govern and avoid demagogic promises or impossible dreams. If, in order to win an election, I needed to make a false promise, it would be preferable to lose and continue my political-pedagogical militancy, persevering in my ethical position.

It is fundamental not to give in to the temptation of believing that the ends justify the means, making condemnable agreements and deals with antagonistic forces. If I am progressive, I cannot join forces with those who deny the popular classes a voice. Much needed are agreements among forces that, while different, do not antagonize each other and that can share the responsibility of governing.

It is imperative that my discourse as a candidate not be betrayed by my actions as an elected official. It is important not to give voters the idea that change is easy; change is difficult, but possible. We must insist on the possibility of change in spite of difficulties.

The question then lies in determining how to turn difficulties into possibility. For that reason, in the struggle for change, we must be neither solely patient nor solely impatient, but (as noted) patiently impatient. Unlimited patience, one that is never restless, ends up immobilizing transformative action. The same is the case with willful impatience, which demands immediate results from action even while it is still being planned.

The mechanist, solely impatient, denies dialectics even when he claims to be dialectic. The answer is in the balanced dosage of both patience and impatience. The world cannot be transformed without either one, for both are needed.

The absolutely impatient bet exclusively on their will and their decision to fight, not taking into account contrary forces, or the available means for use during the struggle. The absolutely patient, valuing neither the reasons for the struggle nor their right to it, tend to transfer to God the responsibility for addressing human shortcomings. Through different paths, both strengthen the power of the unfair. This is the position of some religious individuals, who dichotomize *worldliness* and *transcendentalism*. Along these lines, the more we make the world into a vale of tears (where, by praying and forgiving those who have sinned against us today, we will earn our heaven tomorrow), the more our lives on earth will become an effective way of purging our guilt. It is very easy for those who make money, eat, dress, enjoy music, travel, and have social prestige to ask for patience from those who are denied all that.

I am not against prayer, and I am opposed to the state's exercise of the absurd power of closing down sects or churches, silencing voices, imposing behaviors. However, I refuse to accept this mind-narrowing form of religion. The prayer that believers should engage in, as I see it, is one where they ask God for strength and courage to fight with dedication to overcome injustice.

I have always prayed, asking that God give me increased disposition to fight against the abuses of the powerful against the oppressed. I have always prayed in order that the weakness of the offended would transform itself into the strength with which they would finally defeat the power of the great. I would never ask that God punish those among the violated who rebelled with just rage against the endless evils of the greedy. I have always seen, in the depths of courage of the renegade, even if it was not always very transparent, his ability to love, indispensable to the reinstatement of justice. After all, the oppressed did not initiate oppression, nor did the unloved initiate hatred; rather, they are the primary targets of oppression and hatred.

Mind-narrowing religious behavior supports the exploitation practiced by the rich. It reinforces the discourse of the reactionary who, while religiously indifferent, clasp their hands in prayer to accuse "land squatters, incited by professional subversives, of violating ownership rights and of threatening the peace society requires." Those who wage such accusations never speak of what agrarian reform law represents in Brazil. They never refer to the percentage of those who own land in comparison to those who have nothing. They never say, "How terrible!" at the sight of desperate families who *dine* on hospital waste, pieces of removed breasts, or discarded food in the dump sites of urban centers.

These are people who not only become insensitive to the knowledge of tens of millions of Brazilians dying of starvation, but also accuse the hungry of indolence and incompetence.

Also members of this group are some with more sensitivity who, before the popular requests for improved living conditions, ask restlessly: "What would become of my wife's charity if social justice were made?"

It is people like that we must democratically defeat. People who think of themselves first, of themselves second, and never of others, especially never of those in the popular classes.

Lessons from Exile

One day, forbidden from being, I found myself away from my homeland.

Until 1960, besides Recife, I only knew a few cities in Pernambuco, and I had been for a couple of days in Rio, São Paulo, Florianópolis, and Porto Alegre. The year before the coup, I had been to all Brazilian capitals. I remember how, from North to South, the cities were awake, restless, dreaming of basic reforms, from which this country remains exempt. I remember the verbal incontinence of the Brazilian left, who used to claim a power that they did not have. As a result, they scared the right, leading it to grow stronger and prepare to stage the Coup of 1964.

At times, in one's fight for justice, one neglects seeking a more rigorous knowledge of human beings. One may underestimate the power of the dominant, ignore the deep-seated presence of the oppressor in the oppressed, and end up in exile. Exile is a space–time dimension that one has not chosen, and where one arrives marked by rage, fears, suffering, early longing, love, broken hope, and also by a certain shy hope, one that signals return. There is also the wish and the need to remake oneself, remake one's broken dream.

Exile could not be solely a nostalgic experience, a parenthesis without any reference to tomorrow's return. It imposed itself as a time for revision and development, even to those who intended to return as if they had never left.

Even for those who can quickly resolve their matters of survival, exile is not simply a time to be lived, but one to be *suffered*. It is not possible to suffer such a time without living it; only when one lives this time as an existential experience, can one suffer it. That is why only men and women can be exiled.

I will never forget a comment by the president of Guinea Bissau at the time, Luiz Cabral, during a helicopter ride from the countryside to the capital. While looking at the forest, and seeing some bird move across the sky, he said, "I hope, comrade Paulo, that our animals may soon return from exile."

He was speaking metaphorically. Threatened by war, the animals in his country had sought other *support systems*. None of them had a planned return, and from the human point of view, none had suffered their distance from that support system.

Suffering exile is more than knowing the reality of it. It requires embracing it with all the pain this embrace represents; this is the only way the exiled can prepare for the return. Suffering exile is accepting the tragedy of rupture, which characterizes the experience of existing in a *borrowed context*. One suffers exile as one deals better with the difficulties associated with being unable to return to one's origin. One suffers exile as one reconciles the contradictions between the present where one lives, in a space where one has experienced no past, and the future, which has to be built in uncertain space.

Suffering exile implies recognizing that one has left his or her context of origin; it means experiencing bitterness, the clarity of a cloudy place where one must make right moves to get through. Exile cannot be suffered when it is all pain and pessimism. Exile cannot be suffered when it is all reason. One suffers exile when his or her conscious body, reason, and feelings—one's whole body—is touched by it. I am not reduced to grieving alone, to have a project for the future. I do not live only in the past. Rather, I exist in the present, where I prepare myself for the possible return.

Some in exile, however, become bitter and never imagine any possibility of return. In their constant grief, they neither truly engage themselves in the borrowed context, something that could result in a certain preoccupation with their context of origin, nor correctly dream about the return. They lament exile so much that they are not able to endure it.

I met some exiles who, bitter and sad, remained loyal to the political dream responsible for their uprooting. I cannot remember a single one who had regretted the utopia he or she had fought and been exiled for.

There are also naive optimists, who announce the date of the return every week, along with the fall of the oppressive regime. The day comes and goes, no return, and almost unconsciously, they set another date, which again never comes. And they go on afraid of accepting the truth of their reality.

One thing can be easily realized in the circumstance of exile: how virtues and flaws become highlighted. While a limited situation, exile is provoking. It is impossible to go through it without being tested in your ability to love or feel anger, your ability to tolerate the different, to hear and to respect them.

I met some exiled who believed themselves to possess superior qualities. It was as if they were special beings on almost impossible missions that launched them above all those who remained in the *mediocrity* of their daily existence in their context of origin. They, then, saw themselves as creditors of eternal gratitude from the ones who stayed, who could not even imagine the exiled were fighting for their freedom.

Once in Geneva, an exile told me that, in Brazil, he had experienced the sensation of having been chosen when once, in clandestinity, while walking on a street bustling with people, he said to himself, "Poor men and women, little do they know about their condition of being exploited, and they can't even imagine that here, incognito, I am their savior." *Listening to himself* engaged in such discourse, he told me, he returned to the world. He asked for forgiveness from the people for thinking such an absurdity and saved himself from the arrogance he could have taken on in exile.

One of the things that the exiled, especially the chosen ones, rarely think about is that there is another exile at times as difficult as their own: that of the ones who stay. There is nothing mellow about the exile of the ones who stay, whether because they could not leave the country, or because they heroically refused to move away from their land and culture. There is nothing mellow about the insecurity in which they live, the sleepless nights, the startled awakenings with every car that hits the brake in the neighborhood, the almost certain presence of undercover agents at the service of repression within the university environment, the uneasiness of having to be restrained and only speak in half-truths. What to say about the uncertainty of this half-freedom where, from whisper to whisper, one learns of the fall of another fellow, the repressor closing in further and further?

For all these reasons, as we think of the "internal exiled," it is important to give them credit for something: we were able to return much more as a function of their struggle than as a result of our protests. The role of those who, from out of the country, denounced repression is undeniable, but it would be a primary error to emphasize only the importance of the ones who, from abroad, refused to accept the silence imposed by dictatorship.

The exiled who, once back in Brazil, arrogantly intended to teach those who stayed, instead of relearning Brazil with them, would be incurring error.

In my case, I made an effort to understand, from the perspective of someone coming from abroad, the analyses concerning the country made by those who stayed. I would compare my reading from afar to that of the ones who, up close and with no gaps, had their context as a text. In this relearning of Brazil, my experiences as an exile were of great value: my meetings with others in exile and my experiences around the world, described in *Pedagogy of Hope.*

Each person in exile reacts, suffers, grows, and overcomes difficulties in a different way. Each exiled person experiences exile in his or her own way. Only one thing is the same for all exiles: they find themselves in a borrowed context. The way they exist in this context, and how they deal with their uprooting, depends on a number of internal and external factors: the exile's political choice, which may be more or less clear, the coherence between their progressive discourse and their practice, at times reticent, and their ability to educate their longing, their homesickness, so it does not drag into nostalgia.

I met some exiles who virtually immobilized themselves, who could not manage surviving away from their world unless they made their entire bodies, feelings, fears, desires, reason, gravitate toward the dream of return. It was as if making speeches about the return and inquiring about the signs and the risks of the return were already a bit like returning. The existential splinters that made them suffer away from Brazil were somewhat smoothed out and softened through those speeches. In some almost delirious conversations about the return, I could notice how their permanence in exile was becoming less and less viable. What they refused to accept, however, was not the country where they were, but the circumstance they found themselves in. It was exile itself that kept them from exercising their most basic right: that of returning home. For those in exile who dealt well with the tension brought on by the forbidden return, listening to that nostalgic discourse posed a problem: on the one hand, they could not encourage unreal analyses on the part of their fellow exiles, on the other, they felt uncomfortable to disenchant them.

It was necessary to find pathways leading to disagreement with their naively optimistic diagnosis, through which one would not completely unveil the unfeasibility of the return at that given time. The way was to help them accept exile as an irrefutable, limited situation. It was to help them overcome the state that they found themselves in: they became so anguished in exile that they kept themselves from suffering it.

There was one day, during my exile, when I experienced the bitterness of hopelessness that I had always tried to keep away from myself. News about advances in the struggle for amnesty within Brazil had become more and more frequent. A "democratic opening" marched on and, with it, at a given moment, our return seemed evident. It was a matter of days. If before, in critical terms, the return was not viable, at that point, on the contrary, it was almost certain. If before I could and I should not surrender before the impossibility of return, now, tantalized with the almost-certainty of the return *home*, it became extremely difficult to accept that a reunion with my world could not take place! Released, my longing and homesickness made me more vulnerable.

It was June of 1979, if my memory serves correctly. I was home in the morning when the phone rang. A Brazilian journalist, from Paris, asked if I had already heard that my name was on a list publicized by the Brazilian Ministry of Foreign Affairs of the ten Brazilian exiles who were barred from returning. Ten minutes later, from Bern, Swiss National Radio put the same question, asking me to comment on my reaction.

Taken by indistinguishable emotion, I said that I first had to obtain confirmation. I was concerned about the consequences of commenting on a case that I was not sure I was a part of.

I felt as if I had been walking along a plain when, all of a sudden, I found myself on the edge of a cliff, or as if, after having fought with the waves all night, I had died on the beach at dawn. Never, had I felt the fragility of my uprooting so strongly.

A few days later, I received two newspaper clippings from Brazil. One of them listed my name alongside those of nine other "nonamnestiables," such as: Luiz Carlos Prestes, Miguel Arraes, Leonel Brizola, and Márcio Moreira Alves. In the other news piece, the spokesperson for the Planalto Palace contradicted the information. I recovered strength. In the first few days of August 1979 we landed at Viracopos—Elza, my first wife, myself, and our children, Joaquim and Lutgardes. The permanent return took place in June of the following year.

"Has the gentleman had problems with the Brazilian government?" the officer asked tactfully, with my passport in his hand. "I do," I answered gently, without arrogance. With a friendly smile, another officer approached, holding one of my books. I understood his gesture and autographed it. We walked across the passport check. It was finally over, both factually and legally, the exile I had gone into at forty-three and was now leaving at fifty-eight.

Was I returning old? No. I was returning lived, matured, tested at different times. I was returning hopeful, motivated to relearn Brazil, to participate in the struggle for democracy and for public school to become popular school gradually, thus becoming less elitist, more critical, more open. I was returning young, in spite of physical appearance, my gray beard, and the thinning hair.

As I write this, at seventy-five, I continue to feel young, declining—not for vanity or fear of disclosing my age—the privileges senior citizens are entitled to, for example, at airports.

The main criterion for evaluating age, youth, and old age cannot be that of the calendar. No one is old just because he or she was born a long time ago or young just because he or she was born a short time ago. People are old or young much more as a function of how they think of the world, the availability they have for curiously giving themselves to knowledge. The search for knowledge should never make us tired, and the acquisition of it should never make us immobile and satisfied. People are young or old much more as a function of the energy and the hope that they can readily put into starting over, especially if what they have done continues to embody their dream, an ethically valid and politically necessary dream. We are young or old to the extent that we tend to accept change or not as a sign of life, rather than embrace *the standstill* as a sign of death.

People are young to the extent that they fight to overcome prejudice. A person would be old, even in spite of being only twenty-two, if he or she arrogantly dismissed others and the world. We gradually become old as we unconsciously begin to refuse *novelty*, with the argument that "in our day things were better." The best time for the young person of twenty-two or seventy is always the one that he or she lives in. Only by living time as best as possible can one live it young.

Deeply living the plots presented to us by social experience and accepting the dramatic nature of reinventing the world and the pathways to youth. We grow old if we believe, as we realize the importance we have gained in our environment, that it is of our own merit. We grow old if we believe this importance lies in ourselves rather than in the relations between ourselves, others, and the world.

Pride and self-sufficiency make us old; only in humility can I be open to the life experience where I both help and am helped. I cannot make myself alone, nor can I do things alone. I make myself with others, and with others, I can do things.

The more youth educators possess, the more possible it will be for them to communicate with youth. The young can help educators maintain their youth while educators can help the young not lose theirs.

Old, as defined here, cannot remake the world; that is up to youth. The ideal, however, is to add, to the readiness of youth that the young possess, the collected *wisdom* of the old who have stayed young.

People are being falsely young when they adopt an irresponsible attitude toward risk, when they take risks purely for the thrill of it. Risk only makes sense when it is taken for a valuable reason, an ideal, a dream beyond risk itself.

There is a horrible way to grow old: objecting to necessary political, economic, and social change, a prerequisite for overcoming injustice. Nevertheless, there is no youth that is exempt from aging fast as it attempts to immobilize history; this is what reaction is about. Reaction and youth are as incompatible as defending life and fearing freedom, which is a way of negating life.

How can we maintain ourselves young if we proclaim that the poor are lazy and that indolence is the cause of their poverty? How can we maintain ourselves young if we discriminate against blacks, women, homosexuals, and workers? Preservation of youth is a demanding process. It does not tolerate incoherence. One cannot be, at the same time, *young* and *racist*, *young* and *macho*, *young* and *abusive*.

If it is possible for old to become young and for young to become old, if a twenty-two-year-old *young person* who has become old can recover youth, a young person at age seventy could, all of a sudden, renounce youth and, tragically, turn old. Such a person would be trading beauty for ugliness, and would refuse his or her previous discourse and action. Awakened from the dream, he or she would then bury utopia and preserve what should be radically changed.

Conservatism is also incompatible with youth. What is in effect cannot be preserved, what is effective stands on its own. Who, for example, would dare to propose a ban on the telephone?

Between radically changing the agrarian structure of the country and maintaining it as is, reactionary action would preserve it. Deep down, the reactionary are the true *subversives*, for they fight to maintain an outdated order. The most advance a reactionary would allow him/herself is *reformism*, a process where reforms are implemented to avoid deeper transformation. In a progressive practice, possible and necessary reforms are implemented to make that transformation viable.

My decided refusal then is of reformism, not reforms. Fighting against reformism is a duty of the progressive, who must use the contradictions of reformist practice to defeat it. A reformist government may encourage advances beyond its purpose through some of its reforms. That reformism may manage to avoid deeper transformation is a historic *possibility*, but so is overcoming reformism another historical possibility.

Thus, the historical-social struggle of ethics, of decision, of departure, of choice and the role of critical conscientization in history acquire paramount importance.

For all these reasons, I must insist and reinsist on critical education. The argument that the teaching of content, deposited in the learner, will sooner or later bring about a critical perception of reality does not convince me. In the progressive perspective, the process of teaching—where the teaching challenges learners to *apprehend* the object, to then learn it in their relations with the world—implies the exercise of critical perception, perception of the object's reason for being. It implies the sharpening of the learner's *epistemological curiosity*, which cannot be satisfied with mere description of the object's concept. I must not *leave* for a random tomorrow something that is part of my task as a progressive educator right now: a critical reading of the world, alongside a critical reading of the word.

A progressive educator must not experience the task of teaching in mechanical fashion. He or she must not merely transfer the profile of the concept of the object to learners. If I teach Portuguese, I must teach the use of accents, subject-verb agreement, the syntax of verbs, noun case, the use of pronouns, the personal infinitive. However, as I teach the Portuguese language, I must not postpone dealing with issues of language that relate to social class. I must not avoid the issue of *class* syntax, grammar, semantics, and spelling. Hoping that the teaching of content, in and of itself, will generate tomorrow a radical intelligence of reality is to take on a controlled position rather than a critical one. It means to fall for a magical comprehension of content, which attributes to it a criticalizing power of its own: "The more we deposit content in the learners' heads, and the more diversified that content is, the more possible it will be for them to, sooner or later, experience a critical awakening, decide, and break away."

Any back-alley neoliberal knows very well that such view is absolute nonsense and that he or she would lend his or her support to any educational project where the "reading of the world" was irrelevant.

The "Lefts" and the Right

The political-pedagogical practice of progressive Brazilian educators takes place in a society challenged by economic globalization, hunger, poverty, traditionalism, modernity, and even postmodernity, by authoritarianism, by democracy, by violence, by impunity, by cynicism, by apathy, by hopelessness, but also by hope. It is a society where the majority of voters reveal an undeniable inclination toward change. "The popular majority have been right in deciding what they want, but they have erred in their choice of the partisan forces that they have brought to power," as Ana Maria Freire lucidly analyzes. They were right when they chose change, but they erred when they chose Collor and his entourage.

They want change; they want to win over inflation; they want a strong economy; they want justice, education, and health care for themselves and their families; they want peace in the shanty towns and urban centers; they want to eat and sleep. They want to be happy in a present lived with dignity and in a future whose realization they play a part in. They vote, however, for partisan coalitions, some of whose predominant forces are, by nature, antagonistic to change in favor of the oppressed.

I am certain that the greatest responsibility for such mismatch belongs to the "lefts" themselves. We speak of *the lefts* in the plural and *the right* in the singular. The singularity of the right has to do with the ease with which its different currents unify before danger. Union among the left is always difficult and cumbersome. While the right is only sectarian against progressive thought and practice, the "lefts" are sectarian among themselves. If there are three or four factions within a leftist party, each believes itself to be the only one truly progressive, and they all fight among themselves. Truly leftist-activist members are treated as "the right of the party" or as "managers of the capitalist crisis."

I have no doubt that the radical experience of tolerance is part of the immediate renovation that leftist parties need to undergo if they are to remain historically valid. And here, I speak of a tolerance that must not be confused with status quo. I speak of tolerance in reconciling differing comprehensions of political action by party members, which does not mean lack of principles or discipline. The tolerance that needs to be lived in the intimacy of a leftist political party should transcend its borders. It must not be practiced only among progressive positions within the party, but also between the party and society at large. It should also be effective between the party's leadership and the popular classes, a tolerance made explicit in that leadership's discourse and their practice.

A leftist political party intent on preserving their discourse within an intensely contradictory society such as ours, intent on climbing to power, without which it is not possible *to change* the country, must learn to reread our reality. Learning to reread implies learning a new language. One cannot reread the world if one does not improve the old tools, if one does not reinvent them, if one does not learn to deal with the related parts within the whole one seeks to discover. Likewise, a new reading of my world requires a new language—that of possibility, open to hope. Nowadays we are so vulnerable before unreachable forces—the collision of an asteroid with the earth, the tragedy of AIDS, the possibility of having my little backyard spied on from halfway across the world—hope has become indispensable to our existence. It is difficult to maintain it, hard to reinforce it, but it is impossible to exist without it.

A leftist party cannot engage in a dialogue with the popular classes using outdated language. As it reveals optimism, it must be critical; its hope must not be that of an irresponsible adventurer. Its criticism of the injustice within the capitalist system must be strong. That, though, does not mean this criticism should be pronounced with anger rather than with the goodness and peace characteristic of those engaged in the good combat. This must not be the discourse of bitterness, without even the faintest trace of hope. On the contrary, it must be hopeful, critically optimistic, and "drenched" in ethics.

I can see no reason why progressive activists, men and women, should be careless about their bodies, enemies of beautifulness, as if looking good were an exclusive right of the bourgeois. Today's youth has nothing to do with that: they paint their faces and take to the streets wearing that beautiful joy that also fills their protest.

In search of its renewal, a leftist party must lose any old trace of *avant-gardism*. It must lose any trace of any leadership that decrees itself as the edge, as the final word, one who defines and enlightens. This word necessarily comes from outside the body of the popular classes. Changing from an avant-gardist party to one of the masses alters not only the party's understanding of its role in the history of political struggle, but also its methods and organization, going from a centralism only strategically called *democratic* to decentralization, truly democratic.

The role of activists in an authoritarian, hierarchical party is a very different thing from their duty within a democratic one. In the first instance, the discourse of activists, while members of the party's hierarchy, comes molded by the party's leadership, which is equally molded by its orthodoxy, myths, and absolute truths. In the second instance, the activists' political-pedagogical practice is far from any savior's dream about the "uncultured masses." Their hopeful discourse is not that of someone intending to liberate others, but that of someone inviting others to liberate themselves together. In an authoritarian practice, different activities seek to blindfold the masses and lead them to a *domesticated* future; in a democratic practice, as they expose their reading of the world to popular groups, activists learn with them how the people know.

By learning *how* and *what* the people know, activists can and should teach better what the people already know. They learn with the oppressed the indispensable *ropes* of their resistance, which are, in an elitist view, classified as "flaws of character."

One of the urgent duties of a leftist party in touch with its time is making all its statements, denunciations, and announcements rigorously ethical. It should never accept that lying pays off, nor should it surrender the people's truth to the oppressor. In my prison experience, I never told the colonel who questioned me that I knew communists. I never lost sleep over that either.

Another duty of a progressive party is to struggle, with the most clarity possible, to make popular classes more aware of the problematic nature of the *future*. It is not true that socialism will come because it is announced; it is not true either that socialism collapsed with the Berlin Wall, or that victorious capitalism is an eternal future that has begun. The truth is that the future is created by us, through transformation of the *present*.

Could it be that the present we are living is a good one? Could it be that this is a more or less just present? Could it be that our society has been at least minimally decent? Could it be that we find it possible to sleep while we know tens of millions starve to death? Could it be that we can accept our educational system as reasonable with its current quantitative and qualitative deficiencies? Should we continue to make deals with the World Bank where we spend more than we actually receive? While Secretary of Education in the Erundina administration, I had the fortunate opportunity to decline, politely but categorically, an offer for one of these deals harmful to our country (see "O Banco do Império," an interview with Marília Fonseca by Paulo Moreira Leite, in *Veja* magazine, 11/23/94).

Could it be that lack of respect for public property is a Brazilian way of being that we cannot escape? Could it be that violence, skepticism, and irresponsibility are unchangeable marks of Brazilian nature? No! To change what we presently are it is necessary to change the structures of power radically.

However, no one can do this alone. No political party, no matter how competent and serious, can do this alone. It is not just any old political coalition that will accomplish it either. Only forces that feel equally at home with certain fundamental principles, even though they may have surface differences, can unite for the needed change. How can we expect agrarian reform, even of mediocre grade, from great land owners? How can we expect unstoppable greed to accept limits to its profits? How can we expect the elitist to propose progressive cultural programs and educational projects?

I can imagine how difficult conversation must be, sometimes, between progressives who accept being the right's limit and their new partners. And here I mean not necessarily conversation about government plans, where the difficulties must be even greater. I mean general conversation that brings back memories of past struggles, around the radicalness of their former colleagues in their dream of world transformation.

When the time comes for those progressives to govern, they must either break up with their allies in the right, requiring support from the left, or try some new partisan configuration, or lie to the people once again. That is why I attribute greater responsibility for such discontinuities to the left itself. The difficulty those in the left find in reaching agreement and sorting their differences, which are much less serious than those they have with the right, winds up helping their opposition.

In an interview in the *Folha de São Paulo* newspaper, the famous Mexican anthropologist, Carlos Castanheda, stated, while discussing the left in Latin America, that, in the case of Brazil, it would have been ideal if the configuration of the presidential race in the second round of 1989 had been that of the first round in 1994 (see note 9, page 123).

That would have been, in my view, if the left had already learned to be tolerant, to have historical sensibility, not to claim ownership over the truth. It would have been, if the left had learned the importance of history, the impatiently patient wait. Here I mean a wait where those who wait never settle down, where those who wait more along impatiently patient in carrying out their dreams or projects.

It would have been, if the majority of progressives had already understood that social transformation only really takes place when most of society takes ownership of it and takes the initiative to expand its social radius of acceptance. When transformation is more or less imposed and its implementation is not followed by any effort or explanation about its reason for being, what results is blind obedience, immobilization, passivity, and fear. It may also lead, someday, to uprising.

No one in his right mind would think of a left whose activist force was made up of celestial beings. Politics is a job for concrete men and women, those with flaws and virtues. But one would expect the left to become more coherent, refusing coalitions with its antagonists. One would also demand that the "lefts" overcome their superficial differences, having their common identity as a base.

The democratic, open, critical testimony of progressive leadership before one another has a pedagogical dimension. Undoubtedly, the positions taken by the left, especially those taken by the Workers' Party (PT), have moved the Brazilian political process forward.

For this reason, the right was unable to find any visibility in the presidential race of 1994 other than by decreeing as its limit a man from outside its ranks, one with a political past the right had condemned. If, while having him as its possible limit, the right made him concede more than he should have, it was also forced to take a few steps beyond its natural limits. If the right had chosen a candidate from within its ranks, while the left had remained united, it would not have advanced and would possibly have lost the election.

In this sense, Fernando Henrique Cardoso's victory is as much a result of the Real Plan as of the Brazilian left's struggle, PT included. Logically, added to all that is the president's personality, political skill, and competence.

It is unfortunate that, presently, the advancement experienced by the right is entering undeniable reversal, which, I hope, will not be enough to immobilize popular demands. In order to fight effectively against a possible paralysis, it is necessary that progressive forces be alert and ready to denounce even the smallest attempt to mislead the popular classes.

It is necessary, above all, that the left face some most destructive social infirmities: raging sectarianism, authoritarian messianism, and overflowing arrogance.

In order to stay faithful to my utopia of a less perverse society, I do not need to repeat a discourse that is no longer in line with our times, nor do I need to subscribe to the neoliberal one. As a progressive, I must say *no* to a certain professionalization of the political-partisan practice. It is also indispensable that this practice overcome the voluntary amateurishness of some well-meaning activists. Progressive practice must, however, be kept from sprawling into a mental bureaucracy, one that ties us down to *our* truth, and that we may become enslaved to.

No leftist party can remain faithful to its democratic dream if it falls into the temptation of rallying cries, slogans, prescriptions, indoctrination, and the untouchable power of leaderships. Such temptations inhibit the development of tolerance, in the absence of which democracy is not viable.

No leftist party can remain faithful to its democratic dream if it falls into the temptation of seeing itself as possessing a truth outside which there is no salvation, or if its leadership proclaims itself as the avant-garde edge of the working class.

Any progressive party intent on preserving itself as such, must not lack the ethics of humility, of tolerance, of perservance in the peaceful struggle, of vigor, of an ever-ready curiosity. It must not lack hope with which to restart the struggle whenever necessary. It must not defend the interests of the popular classes, their right to a dignifying life, their right to pronouncing the world, and at the same time look the other way while the taxpayer's money is being stolen. Such a party's coherence must be absolute. A political party is not a monastery of sanctified monks, but it should aspire to become an association of truly serious and coherent people, those who work to shorten more and more the distance between what they say and what they do.

A leftist party intent on bringing itself to meet the demands of its time needs to overcome the old prejudice against anything that resembles a bourgeois concession. It must be able to realize that, at a time as needy for humanization as ours, fighting for *solidarity*, before the negation of even minimal rights suffered by most, is endlessly more valuable than any bureaucratic discourse of ultraleftist flavor.

An authentic progressive party must not become sectarian, for that would represent a move away from its normal radical position. Radicalness is tolerant; sectarianism is blind and antidemocratic. Unlike the sectarian, always tied to their truth, the radical are always open to revising themselves; they are always ready to discuss their positions. The radical are not *intransigent*, even though they can never condone unethical behavior.

Radicalness is serene, so long as it does not fear change when it is needed. That is why the progressive are always open to overcoming. Continuing a discussion and defending a certain argument make no more sense to them if someone can convince them of the opposite. That is not the case with the sectarian, who will continue to defend their position even if convinced of their error. Radicals are at the service of truth; the sectarian at the service of their truth, which they hope to impose.

Sectarization is sterile, is *necrophilic.* Radicalness is creative, *biophilic.* Radicals fight for *purity;* the sectarian will settle for *puritanism*, which is make-believe purity. Never has

Brazil had a deeper need for progressive men and women—serious, radical, engaged in the struggle for transforming society and in giving testimony of their respect for the people.

There is no denying a certain degree of optimism toward the real changes Brazilian society may experience from now on. Overall, there seems to be an atmosphere of hope. It feels like *fatigue at the highest degree*. And that gets added to outrageous pillage of public money, impunity, and you-scratch-my-back-I'll-scratch-your-back politics, one of the most resilient vices in this country.

Even right-wing forces seem a bit intimidated by the indignation felt within Brazilian society. Any chance of the present government's proving to be effective, while a serious project, will depend on that intimidation. But the fundamental changes to the country will not count on the endorsement of the right. And the right did not vote for Fernendo Henrique because he was a lesser evil. Not at all. The right chose him as its *limit*, and he accepted that condition. My hope—which is based on my personal knowledge of him and on his political life history—is that he will go beyond the limits that they hope to force down on him.

As I see it, the true left, one not afraid or ashamed of defining itself as such, should not play the role of betting on the right's success. Instead, the left should focus on undermining the right's importance and its power of influence over governmental decisions. The critical left's role is to realize that, having completed the stage of democratic transition, we now enter another state, that of democratic *intimacy*. Thus far we had been crossing the road between authoritarianism and democracy. Now, already in democracy, we must, on the one hand, reinforce it and, on the other, move forward in the social domain. Whether it had been under Lula, or be it under Fernando Henrique Cardoso, the government embodies this movement.

Not at any time will Brazil have ever needed so much to count on its radicals' engaging in the struggle for deep social transformation, for *unity within diversity*. This expression is made up of two nouns connected by the preposition *within*. It is interesting how, in addition to its characteristic connective function, prepositions presuppose another: to impregnate a phrase with the very meaning of the relationship it embodies. There is a certain kinship between the relationship-meaning of the preposition and the syntactic status of the word that requires it. When I say, "I live on Valença Street," the preposition *on* means *placement*, coinciding with the syntactic status of the verb *to live*, or *to reside*. For this reason, I cannot say, "living to Valença Street." The proposition *to* indicates movement while the status of the word *street*, regarding the verb, requires the preposition of place *on*. It is just as incorrect to say, "I live to Valença Street," as it is to say, "I went on Pedro's house." *To go* is a verb of movement, thus requiring the preposition *to*, not *on*.

If I say *unity within diversity*, it is because, even while I recognize that the differences between people, groups, and ethnicities may make it more difficult to work in unity, unity is still possible. What is more: it is needed, considering that the objectives the different groups fight for coincide. Equality *of* and *in* objectives may make unity possible within the difference. The lack of unity among the reconcilable "different" helps the hegemony of the antagonistic "different." The most important is the fight against the main enemy.

Therefore, the "different" who accept unity cannot forego unity in their fight; they must have objectives beyond those specific ones of each group. There has to be a greater dream, a utopia the different aspire to and for which they are able to make concessions. Unity within diversity is possible, for example, between antiracist groups, regardless of the group members' skin color. In order for that to happen, it is necessary for the antiracist groups to overcome the limits of their core racial group and fight for radical transformation of the socioeconomic system that intensifies racism.

The perversity of racism is not inherent to the nature of human beings. We *are* not racist; we *become* racist just as we may stop being that way.

The problem I have with racist people is not the color of their skin, but rather the color of their ideology. Likewise, my difficulty with the *macho* does not rest in their sex, but in their discriminatory ideology. Being racist or macho, progressive or reactionary, is not an integral part of human nature; rather it is an *orientation toward being more*. And that orientation is incompatible with any sort of discrimination.

If I am certain that the only kind of prejudice that can be fully explained by class analysis is the prejudice of class, I also know that the class factor is hidden within both sexual and racial discrimination. We cannot reduce all prejudice to a classist explanation, but we may not overlook in understanding the different kinds of discrimination.

When a so-called minority refuses to join forces with another minority, it reveals a prejudiced certainty: that of the other's natural inability to be fair and decent. I do not understand how, in Brazil, we can maintain feminist, black, Indian, working-class groups separately struggling for a less perverse society. Each group is fighting its own battles.

Unity within diversity is an imposition of the very fight. The dominant know that very well. Thus, one of their golden rules is, "divide to govern." We, who are classified by them as minorities, take on this profile. Therefore, we tend to divide forces fighting among and against ourselves, instead of fighting the common enemy.

Tolerance reveals excessive self-valuation on the part of the intolerant in relation to others, who are considered by the intolerant to be inferior, to their class, their race, their group, their sex, their nation. For this reason, there is no tolerance within a lack of humility. How can one be tolerant if one considers others to be inferior? But one cannot be humble by bureaucratically doing favors to others. In order to be humble, one must be so in practice as one enters relationships with others. One is not humble by underestimating others or overestimating oneself.

The oppressor is not humble, but arrogant. The oppressed is not humble either, but humiliated. In order for oppressor and oppressed to become humble, it is necessary for the oppressor to convert to the cause of the oppressed, and for the oppressed to commit to his own fight for liberation. It is only from that point on that both will have met the requirements to learning humility.

Theories considering liberation as a given fact of history, or basing it exclusively on scientific knowledge, never excited me very much. The same goes for those that did not accept giving any serious consideration, for example, to human nature, even if human nature was understood to be socially and historically constituted. I mean human nature while taking place in history, rather than prior to history. I cannot think the issue of liberation, and all that it implies, without thinking about human nature.

The possibility of discerning comparing, choosing, programming, performing, evaluating, commiting, taking risks, makes us beings of decision and, thus, ethical beings. For this reason, fighting against discrimination is an ethical imperative. Whether discriminated against for being black, female, homosexual, working class, Brazilian, Arabic, Jewish—regardless of the reason—we have the obligation to fight against discrimination. Discrimination offends us all, for it hurts the substantiveness of our being.

Our fight against the different discriminations, against any negation of our being, will only lead to victory if we can realize the obvious: *unity within diversity*. And by unity I mean that of the reconcilable different, not of the antagonically different. Among the latter, in the process of the struggle, there may be a pact as a function of circumstantial objectives serving both extremes. Among the former, unity is based on strategic and not only tactic objectives.

The appropriateness of my discourse might be questioned, for I speak as an activist when I should speak as theoretician and vice versa. I reject such dichotomy: I am not a theoretician, say on Wednesdays, and an activist on Saturdays.

The criticism of capitalism I put forth, from an ethical point of view, derives as much from the educator as it does from the activist, which I seek to continue to be in my own way. My activism can never become dissociated from my theoretical work; on the contrary, the former has its tactics and strategies formulated on the latter. The moment we recognize that food production around the world could be sufficient to feed twice its population, it is desolating to realize the numbers of those who come into the world but do not stay, or those who do but are forced into early departure by hunger.

My struggle against capitalism is founded on that—its intrinsic perversity, its antisolidarity nature.

The argument has been destroyed of scarcity as a production problem that capitalism would not be able to respond to and that would represent an obstacle to the preservation of this system. Capitalism is effective in this and other aspects, but it has shown its other face—absolute insensitivity to the ethical dimension of existence.

It has produced scarcity within abundance and need within plenty. Thus, the neoliberal feel the need to impregnate their discourse with a fatalism, to them irrefutable, according to which "things are the way they are because there is no other way."

This cynical discourse tends to convince that the problem lies in destiny or fate, rather than severely criticize a system that, in spite of lack of scarcity, condemns a large part of humanity to hunger and death. Successive technological revolutions have rendered capitalism bare. They have forced it to expose its own evil—millions of people dying from starvation, head-to-head with wealth.

I refuse, for all these reasons, to think that we are eternally destined to live the negation of our own selves. In order to be in the world, my conscious body, my unfinished and historical being, needs food as much as it needs ethics. The fight would make no sense to me without this ethics backdrop, upon which experiences of comparison, criticism, choice, decision, and rupture take place.

I would be a melancholy and unmotivated being if it could be scientifically proved that the laws of history or nature would take care of surpassing human misencounters without any mark of freedom: as if everything were predetermined, preestablished, as if this were a world without errors or mistakes, without alternatives. Error and mistakes imply the adventure of the spirit. Such adventure does not take place where there is no space for freedom. There is only error when the individual in error is conscious of the world and of himself or herself in the world, with himself or herself and with others; there is only error when whoever errs can know he or she has erred because he or she knows that he or she does *not* know. At last, in this process, error is a temporary form of knowing.

At the very moment I write these lines, I am reminded of Berenger, Ionesco's character. His cries of refusal to become a rhinoceros are a powerful testimony to our rebelliousness, our affirmation as men and women in the exercise of our citizenship, in the struggle for the millions deprived of it.

Seriousness and Happiness

There is much talk today, not only in Brazil, about education and citizenship. There is talk about fighting for democracy, about the active involvement of the popular classes in shaping the destiny of cities. I would like to make it clear that it is not possible to make Brazilian society more and more democratic without starting by attacking hunger, unemployment, the health crisis, and that of education. The solution to these problems implies redefining the role of the state, moving away from an economistic comprehension of development, and instituting an educational practice coherent with democratic values.

An educational practice must be instituted that proposes and takes advantages of situations where the learners may experience the power and the value of unity within diversity. It should do nothing to stimulate lack of solidarity and fellowship. It should do nothing that works against the development of serious discipline of body and mind, without which all efforts for knowledge fail. It must do everything to ensure an atmosphere in the classroom where teaching, learning, and studying are serious acts, but also ones that generate happiness. Only to an authoritarian mind can the act of educating be seen as a dull task. Democratic educators can only see the acts of teaching, of learning, of studying as serious, demanding tasks that not only generate satisfaction but are pleasurable in and of themselves.

The satisfaction with which they stand before the students, the confidence with which they speak, the openness with which they listen, and the justice with which they address the students' problems make the democratic educator a model. Their authority is affirmed without disrespect of freedom. It is affirmed for this very reason. Because they respect freedom, they are respected. A democratic educator cannot allow his or her authority to become atrophied, for that would exacerbate the learners' freedom. He or she cannot contradict himself or herself in favor of his or her authority, nor in favor of the learners' freedom: neither authoritarianism nor permissiveness.

The power of a democratic educator lies in exemplary coherence; that is what sustains his or her authority. An educator who says one thing and does another is irresponsible, and not only ineffective but also harmful. He or she is more of a disservice than a coherent authoritarian.

An educator's authoritarianism is not only manifested in the repressive use of authority, which restricts the movements of the learners. It is equally manifested in a number of opportunities, in his or her excessive vigilance over the learners, in his or her lack of respect for the learners' creativity, and for his or her cultural identity. It is also manifested in his or her lack of acceptance of the popular-class learners' way of being, the manner in which he or she warns the students and censures them. An educator's authoritarianism is also manifested in his or her narrow understanding of the teach/learn equation, within which the learners are restricted to the mechanical memorization of what the educator deposits in them. That is the "banking educator," as I termed him or her in *Pedagogy of the Oppressed*.

Today in Brazil, we are, perhaps more than yesterday, in need of an exemplary democratic educational practice. We need campaigns implemented, for example, through democracy-studies weeks in public and private schools, universities, vocational schools, unions. We need campaigns that could flood our cities with democracy. They would present the history of democracy and allow for debates on the relationship between democracy and ethics, democracy and popular classes, democracy and economics. They would also focus on elections and the rights and obligations they imply. They would focus on the Brazilian lack of democratic experience, on democracy and tolerance. A taste for freedom and democracy; irreconcilably contradictory forces, reconcilably different forces; unity within diversity.

I do not mean to sound as if I suddenly believed that democracy could be taught through speeches. Democracy is taught and learned through the practice of democracy. It is possible and necessary, however, to discuss the presence or absence of a democratic practice, the reasons for being, for example, of our democratic inexperience.

Brazilian society has enough historical experience with the betrayal of democracy and with democratic rebelliousness upon which to build discussion that can strengthen the latter **(see note 10, page 126)**.

The practice of simulated elections for president and governor is already common, especially in private urban schools.

Through this process, the learners gradually acquaint themselves with political struggle, the positions of political parties, and their ethical demands.

Dialogism

I now return to the discussion of a dialogic relationship, while a fundamental practice to human nature and to democracy on the one hand, and on the other, as an epistemological requirement.

As a matter of method, I never directly focus my attention on the object that challenges me in the process of knowledge discovery. On the contrary, by taking epistemological distance from the object, I proceed to approach it by encircling it. "Takign epistemological distance" means taking the object in hand in order to get to know it; in my "epistemological encircling" of it, I seek to decipher some of its reasons for being in order to appropriate its substantiveness better. In the epistemological encircling, I do not intend to isolate the object to apprehend it; in this operation, I try to understand the object, the interior of its relationship with others.

This is how I will work through the issue of *dialogism.* Instead of describing a profile of the concept of dialogism, I will begin by attempting to comprehend its foundation, what makes of it a strategic requirement, rather than solely the tactics of "smart" subjects toward reaching results. Dialogism must not be understood as a tool used by the educator, at times, in keeping with his or her political choices. Dialogism is a requirement of human nature and also a sign of the educator's democratic stand.

There is no communication without dialogism, and communication lies at the core of the vital phenomenon. In this sense, communication is life and a vector for *more-life.* But, if communication and information occur on the level of life upon its support, let us imagine its importance and, thus, that of dialogism for human existence in the world. On this level, communication and information are served by sophisticated languages and by technological instruments that "shorten" space and time. The social production of language and of instruments with which human beings can better interfere in the world announce what technology will be.

Not too long ago, my grandson, Alexandre Dowbor, called me to say that his computer, connected to the Internet, had "picked up" a message from a German scholar requesting my address. He responded to her request and also provided my fax number. Fifteen minutes later, I was talking with the German professor: thanks to technology.

If my mother, who died in 1978, had been back to the earth for a moment and listened to my conversation with Alexandre, she would have understood nothing.

I have called attention to human nature as *being* socially and historically *constituted*, rather than as preexisting. The trajectory through which we make ourselves conscious is marked by finiteness, by inconclusion, and it characterizes us as historical beings.

Not only have we been unfinished, but we have made ourselves capable of knowing ourselves as such. Here, an opportunity is open for us to become immersed in a permanent search. One of the roots of education, which makes it specifically human, lies in the radicalness of an inconclusion that is perceived as such. The permanence of education also lies in the constant character of the search, perceived as necessary. Likewise, here lie also roots of the metaphysical foundation of hope. How would it be possible for a consciously inconclusive being to become immersed in a permanent search without hope? My hope starts from my nature as a project. For this reason I am hopeful, and not for pure stubbornness.

In order for finiteness, which implies a process, a claim for education, it is necessary that the being involved becomes aware of it. Consciousness of one's inconclusiveness makes that being educable. Unfinishedness in the absence of consciousness about it engenders *domestication* and *cultivation*. Animals are domesticated; plants are cultivated; men and women educate themselves.

Consciousness of, an intentionality of consciousness does not end with rationality. Consciousness about the world, which implies consciousness about myself in the world, with it and with others, which also implies our ability to realize the world, to understand it, is not limited to a rationalistic experience. This consciousness is a totality—reason, feelings, emotions, desires; my body, conscious of the world and myself, seizes the world toward which it has an intention.

My *conscious body's* constant exercise in releasing itself *even to* or *from* my consciousness intending toward the world brings or contains in itself a certain quality of life that, in the human existence, becomes more intense and richer. I am referring to the need for *relational* experience on the level of *existence* and of *interactions*, the level of *living*.

There is a fundamental element in *interaction*, which takes on greater complexity in *relationship*. I am referring to *curiosity*, some sort of openness to comprehending what is in the orbit of the challenged being's sensibility. It is this human disposition to be surprised before people, what they do, say, seem like, before facts and phenomena, before beauty and ugliness, this unrefrainable need to understand in order to explain, to seek the reason for being of facts. It is this desire, always alive, of feeling, living, realizing what lies in the realm of one's "visions of depth" (see *Pedagogy of the Oppressed*, New Revised 20th-Anniversary Edition, New York: Continuum, 1993).

Without the curiosity that makes us beings in permanent availability for questioning—be the questioning well constructed or poorly founded, it does not matter—there would be no gnoseologic activity, a concrete expression of our possibility of knowing.

Concern with the mechanical memorization of content is curious, the use of repetitive exercises that surpass a reason-

able limit while leaving out *a critical education about curiosity*
(see Paulo Freire and Antonio Faundez, *Learning to Question*,
New York: Continuum, 1989). We continue to discourse about
answers and questions that were not posed to us, without emphasizing the importance of curiosity to the students.

Let us take half a day in Pedro's life as the object of our
curiosity. Let us follow his main movements: he awakes,
showers, eats breakfast. He skims the first pages of the newspaper, and since he lives near the university where he works,
he walks over there. He leaves the house, greets some people,
walks past others; carefree, he observes the rushed movement
of those coming and going; he says good morning to some,
smiles at others. At the sight of a WALK sign, he walks across
to the other side. He runs into a friend, detains himself. It is
a short conversation, promises of meeting again, who knows,
maybe next Wednesday. They know they are not going to meet
then. The promises will not hurt either one. They will not
expect each other next Wednesday.

Peter gets to the university. He greets some coworkers and
students. He heads over to the room where the Tuesday seminars are held.

So far, from the moment of his morning shower to his arrival at the seminar room, Pedro has not once questioned himself about this or that action of his. His mind is not
epistemologically operating. This is what characterizes our
movement through the world of day-to-day life.

That does not mean to say that there may not be curiosity
in day-to-day life. It exists and it could not not exist: there we
have it, human life, existence. In this domain, however, our
curiosity is *unguarded*, spontaneous, without any methodical
rigor. It does not lack method, for there cannot be curiosity
without method: it is methodical in itself.

There is another way to immerse ourselves pleasurably in
a challenge. It is a matter of aesthetic curiosity. It is what
makes me stop and gaze upon the sunset. It is what detains
me, lost in my contemplation of the speed and elegance with

which the clouds move across the blue depth of the sky. It is what touches me when faced with a work of art that centers me in beauty.

Unguarded curiosity must not be the way for Pedro to behave in the classroom. The seminar room is a *theoretical context*, which is in a contradictory relationship with a *concrete context*, where facts occur; thus, it demands epistemological curiosity. This curiosity, however, does not refuse to consider the aesthetic. On the contrary, it avails itself of it.

In a theoretical context, we take distance from the concrete one in order, while objectifying it, to examine what takes place in it critically. In a concrete context, there is always the possibility of its subjects' adopting a reflective-critical position; in it, spontaneous curiosity may come to be epistemological.

If, while engaged in concreteness, I could not distance myself from it in order to understand it better only because I found myself in action, the relationship between the concrete context and the theoretical one would be solely mechanical. In order to reflect theoretically upon my practice, it is not required that I change physical contexts. It is required that my curiosity become epistemological. The appropriate context for the exercise of epistemological curiosity is the theoretical one. But physical space is not what makes a context theoretical, the state of the mind is. That being, hence, how we may convert a given moment in the concrete context into a theoretical moment.

Likewise, the space of the concrete context does not necessarily make it theoretical, but the epistemologically curious posture with which we may operate in it does. In the same way, the methodological rigor indispensable to the theoretical context may be twisted, leading one to operate mechanically in that context. The *banking* model of educational practice is of this kind.

Spontaneous curiosity is not what makes it possible to take epistemological distance. This task belongs to epistemological curiosity—overcoming naive curiosity, it makes itself more methodically rigorous. It is this methodical rigor that takes knowledge from the level of *common sense* to that of scientific knowledge. Scientific knowledge is not what is rigorous. Rigor lies in the method applied in an approach to the object. This rigor allows for a greater or lesser *precision* in the knowledge produced or found through our epistemological quest.

As we emphasize an epistemologically curious posture as fundamental in constituting the theoretical context, the importance of this space should be clear. Due attention to the educational space, while it is a context open to the exercise of epistemological curiosity, should be a concern of every serious educational project.

Attention should go into every detail of the school space: hygiene, wall furnishings, cleanliness of desks, the teacher's desk setup, educational materials, books, magazines, newspapers, dictionaries, encyclopedias, and little by little, the introduction of projectors, video, fax, computers. By making clear that the educational space is valuable, the administration is able to demand the due respect for it from learners. Further, this is the way to facilitating the exercise of epistemological curiosity. Without that, the progressive educational practice deteriorates.

While a practice of learning and teaching, educational practice is gnoseologic by nature. The role of the progressive educator is to challenge the learner's naive curiosity in order that they can both share criticalness. That is how an educational practice can affirm itself as the unveiling of hidden truths.

I have previously mentioned the mistake of the postmodernist, who before such contemporary demands as responsiveness to different situations, must defend a certain variety of critical education. To them, however, such education must not go beyond the administrative and technical domains, which are seen as neutral.

The pragmatic reactionary educator who teaches biology, for example, sees no reason to challenge the learner to discuss the vital phenomenon from a social, ideological, or political point of view. What is strictly necessary for them is to deposit contents about the vital phenomenon in the learner.

A technicistic vision of education, which renders it purely technical, or worse yet neutral, works toward the instrumental *training* of the learner. It assumes that there is no longer any antagonism between interests, that everything is more or less the same, and that all that really matters is solely technical training, the standardization of content, and the transfer of a well-behaved *knowledge of results.*

Within such political vision, the permanent development of educators will adhere too much to the *banking* model. The enlightened professional development committees will be interested in training front-line educators—reduced to the role of subordinate intellectuals—into using teaching techniques and materials designed to transfer the "indispensable" content (see Henry Giroux, *Teachers as Intellectuals—Toward a Critical Pedagogy*).

Well to the liking of the World Bank, this political vision necessarily ignores the intelligence and judgment and creative abilities of teachers. Teachers need to be respected, decently paid, called into discussions of their problems, the local, regional, and national problems woven into the problems of education. They must not be diminished and blamed for the gaps in their professional development (see note 11, page 138).

Let us overcome the gaps, but not from the starting point of raising the proclaimed incompetence of teachers. It would be extraordinary if—given our historic situation of disrespect toward public problems, toward teachers, with the starving salaries that they receive—the majority of them *did not* result in desperation (see note 12, page 139).

We shall overcome the gaps by redirecting public spending, eliminating wasteful spending, and eradicating contempt for public property, through an effective fiscal policy, and by revising the role of the state. From all that, the concrete possibility will result in a pedagogical policy based on the decent treatment of teachers and on the exercise of their legitimate development. Only from this point on will it be possible to demand effectiveness from teachers.

Let us return to the issue of dialogism in relation to naive and epistemological curiosity. A dialogic relationship—communication and intercommunication among active subjects who are immune to the bureaucratization of their minds and open to discovery and to knowing more—is indispensable to knowledge. The social nature of this process makes a dialogical relationship a natural element of it. In that sense, authoritarian antidialogue violates the nature of human beings, their process of discovery, and it contradicts democracy.

Authoritarian regimes are enemies of curiosity. They punish citizens for displaying it. Authoritarian power is prying, not curious or questioning. Dialogue, on the other hand, is full of curiosity and unrest. It is full of mutual respect between the dialoging subjects. Dialogism presupposes maturity, a spirit of adventure, confidence in questioning, and seriousness in providing answers. In a dialogic atmosphere, the questioning subject knows the reason for being the questioner. They do not ask questions just for asking or just to seem *alive* to the listener.

A dialogic relationship is the mark of a gnoseologic process: it is not a favor or kindness. Dialogic seriousness and surrender to a critical quest must not be confused with *babbling*. To dialogue is not to babble. That is why there may be dialogue in a professor's critical, rigorously methodical exposition, to which the learners' listen as if *to eat up* the discourse, but also to understand its intellection.

Even though things are never just their atmosphere, but are things themselves, we may speak of a *dialogic atmosphere.* There is an invisible, previous dialogue where one does not need *to make up* questions. Truly democratic educators *are not* for the moment, but *are* by nature dialogic. One of their substantive tasks in our society is to gestate this dialogic atmosphere.

Dialogic experience is fundamental for building epistemological curiosity. Dialogue also implies a critical posture; it implies a preoccupation with the raison d'être of the objects that mediates the subjects of the dialogue.

The growing gap between educational practice and the epistemological curiosity exercise is of concern to me. I fear the curiosity achieved by an educational practice reduced to pure technique may be an anesthetized curiosity, one that does not go past a *scientificist* position before the world.

This is what lies at the core of the "pragmatic" discourse about education. The utopia of solidarity makes way for technical training directed toward survival in a world without dreams, "which have created enough problems." In this case, what matters is training learners just so they can *manage* well.

What counts is training them so that they can adapt without protest. Protest agitates, undermines, twists the truth; it disrupts and moves against order, against the *silence* needed from those who produce.

I reject this fatalism in the name of my understanding of the human being and of history, of my ethical point of view and, because I cannot deny it, of my faith. Here and in other writings, I have spoken about how I understand the human being and history. I would like to emphasize the *finiteness* we are aware of that makes us beings inserted in a permanent search for *being more*—both the natural inclination and the risk of losing *direction* at the same time. Our historical inclination is not fate, but rather possibility. And there cannot be possibility that is not exposed to its negation, to impossibility. Conversely, something impossible today may come to be possible some day. In history as possibility we cannot be but responsible, thus ethical. Such responsibility implies an equally ethical struggle so that we can live up to it. The fact that we are ontologically responsible is not something that can be experienced without search, without fighting against those who irresponsibly prohibit us from being responsible for our own freedom. For this reason, the struggle for liberation implies a previous task, that of accepting the very struggle only as we stand for it. That is how we liberate ourselves, or fail to. Freedom, without which we cannot be, is not a gift but a conquest.

The statement, "Things are as they are because they cannot be any other way," is one of the many instruments used by the dominant in an attempt to abort the dominated's *resistance*. The more historically anesthetized, the more fatalistically immersed in a reality impossible to be touched, let alone transformed, the less of a future we have. Hope is pulverized in the immobility of a crushing present, some sort of final stop beyond which nothing is possible *(Pedagogy of Hope)*.

My Faith and Hope

Some time ago, I had lunch with an American woman religious and two homeless people in San Francisco. Our conversation was interspersed with hopelessness throughout. "Once on the streets, you can never get out. What else could I offer you besides my desolation? The days go by. The nights are consumed and I feel crushed inside them. It has been a long time since I have had a ray of light make a crack in my days and nights. At first, my hope resided in dreams. I used to think that I could experience some happiness while I was sleeping," said one of them with a distant gaze. It was the same expression in the eyes of the country boy from São Paulo who only had nightmares. In any case, the nights of that homeless person seemed better, "I can dive into them and drown my pain."

My ethical and political responsibility does not allow me to hesitate before the cynicism of those who say, "Things are as they are because there is no other way." If I settled for the lie in this phrase, I would be betraying the desperate in the world, like that one in San Francisco. I do not know his name. I never saw him again. If he still lives, on the bottom of time, he will probably not read this text. He will not know how much he helped me by speaking about his impotence, which he made critically clear as he described his tragic experience: falling on the streets without ever being able to return.

Two or three days after that lunch, I visited a Catholic house in San Francisco where poor and relegated people received help. A white woman, frazzled and with difficulty in articulating her speech, looked at me. "You are American, aren't you?" With teary eyes, a suffered sparkle, she answered: "No! I am *poor.*" That was the first time I heard poverty used as a nationality. Feeling guilty, rather accepting the guilt the system has attributed her for her lack of success, she said she was not American. In her self-incrimination, it was as if she begged for forgiveness from *Americanness* for not having a successful existence. That desolate woman expressed, in a very significant way, the absence of citizenship in her. She had been expelled from existence itself. This is the extraordinary power of ideology. That woman had introjected it to such a degree that, as she spoke, it was as if it were not her any longer, but ideology itself that spoke. Her discourse manifested the dominant ideology that inhabited her to the point that she was all self-criticism.

I thought: "If we were in a trial, this poor woman would be the defendant and her own prosecutor at the same time. She'd have no defense."

Her guilt inhibited her the same way a fatalist posture would. The fatalism of the poor undeniably helps only the dominant. We are tempted to think that fatalism is an invention of the dominant to impede rebellion from the dominated, or to put it off as much as possible. We are tempted to think of it as an invention whose engineering is discussed in the offices of dominant leaders. It is not quite like that: the fabric of the oppressive situation is what generates a fatalistic understanding of the world, of a God strangely loving toward its children, for it tests them with pain, need, and misfortune. Generating itself in the oppressive situation and serving it, fatalism is nourished by the oppressors. The comprehension of a God that punishes rebelliousness against injustice and blesses resigned acceptance of antilove is natural to fatalism.

The situation that generates such intelligence of the world and of God does not offer those immersed in it any way out other than settling for their own pain. Becoming *unsettled*, indicating any doubt about the legitimacy of that situation would mean a sin against the will of God. Supported by the historic anesthesia of the suffering and patient populations, the dominant use God to their ends.

The issue around liberation and its practice is not fighting against the religiousness of the popular classes, which is a right of theirs and an expression of their culture, but rather overcoming, *with* it, the vision of a God at the service of the strong for a God on the side of those with whom justice, truth, and love should be. What marked popular religiousness—resignation and annihilation—would be substituted with forms of resistance to outrage, to perversity.

This way, submission-faith toward a destiny that would reflect God's will makes way for a spurring faith of loving rebelliousness. In this process, there is an understanding of the body—for those who have evolved in their faith—as the dwelling of sin turns into an intelligence of the body as the temple of God.

When I defend unity within diversity, I am thinking of unity between those who live their liberating faith and those who do not have it, regardless of why.

I cannot see how those who so live their faith could negate those who do not live it, and vice versa. If our utopia is the constant changing of the world and the overcoming of injustice, I cannot refuse the contribution of progressives who have no faith, nor can I be rejected for having it. What must not be accepted in those who proclaim their faith is that they *use* it at the service of the popular classes' uncriticalness.

This is how I have always understood God—a presence in history that does not preclude me from making history, but rather pushes me toward world transformation, which makes it possible to restore the *humanity* of those who exploit and of the weak.

One of the positives among all the negativity of the troubles my family faced was having gone through the crisis that we did without being tempted to adopt a fatalistic position. Far from us was the idea that we were being tested by God. On the contrary, early on I found myself convinced of the need to change the world, to repair what seemed wrong to me. This attitude was more like a *premonition*, intuition, than absolute knowledge (see *Letters to Cristina*, 1996).

I do not feel very comfortable speaking about my faith. At least, I do not feel as comfortable as I do when speaking about my political choice, my utopia, and my pedagogical dreams. I do want to mention, however, the fundamental importance of my faith in my struggle for overcoming an oppressive reality and for building a less ugly society, one that is less evil and more humane.

All arguments in favor of the legitimacy of my struggle for a more *people-oriented* society have their deepest roots in my faith. It sustains me, motivates me, challenges me, and it has never allowed me to say, "Stop, settle down; things are as they are because they cannot be any other way."

Still young, I read in Miguel de Unamuno that "ideas are to be had; beliefs are for one to be in." I am in my faith, but because it does not immobilize me, being in faith means moving, engaging in different forms of action coherent with that faith. It is to engage in action that *reaffirms* it and never action that *negates* it. *Negating* faith is not being without it, but rather *contradicting* it through acts. Not having faith is both a possibility and a right of human beings, who cease to be human if they are denied their freedom to believe or not believe. Having faith, believing, is not the problem; the problem is claiming to have it and, at the same time, contradicting it in action.

In that sense, coherence and a taste for it are indispensable in building a balance between what I preach and what I do.

To give testimony against one's proclaimed faith is to work against faith.

Since I was a child, I have never been able to understand how it could be possible to reconcile faith in Christ with discrimination on the basis of race, sex, social class, or national origin. How is it possible to "walk" with Christ, but refer to the popular classes as "these stinky people" or "riffraff."

It is not easy to have faith. Above all, it is not easy due to the demands faith places on whoever experiences it. It demands a stand for freedom, which implies respect for the freedom of others, in an ethical sense, in the sense of humility, coherence, and tolerance.

If vigorous faith can authentically emerge among the abused, it is less likely to blossom among the arrogant. In order for those to be touched by faith, they first need to be emptied of the power that makes them all-powerful. So that, humiliated, they may live true faith, they need to assume no humiliation, even if weak, without losing humility.

For this reason, *salvation* implies *liberation*, engagement in a struggle for it. It is as if the fight against exploitation, its motivation, and the refusal of resignation were paths to salvation. The process of salvation cannot be realized without rebelliousness.

It is not easy to have faith.

A friend asked me, as if he already knew the answer, how far my optimism would go before the absurdly high number of daily bank robberies, witness killings, massacres, *Candelarias*, embezzlements, scandals, kidnappings, rapes, scandals in Congress, undue amnesties, the betrayal of the *impeachment* via legal technique.

My friend asked me these questions on the same day that Collor was acquitted in the Supreme Court and the second witness in the Candelaria massacre was killed. My friend had come to hear that, in spite of everything, my hope and my optimism are still alive. His question increased my responsibility because I realized that, in my hope, he was seeking support for his. What he may not have known is that I needed him as much as he needed me. The struggle for hope is permanent, and it becomes intensified when one realizes it is not a solitary struggle **(see note 13, p. 140)**.

If hope is rooted in the inconclusion of a being, something else is needed in order to personify it. It is necessary to accept the *inconclusion* that one becomes aware of. As one does that, one's inconclusion becomes critical, and they may never lack hope again. Critical acceptance of my inconclusion necessarily immerses me in permanent search. What makes me hopeful is not so much the certainty of the *find*, but my movement in *search*. It is not possible to search without hope, not even in solitude.

It is true that the ethical deterioration of Brazilian society has been reaching unbearable levels. But it is also certain that, no matter how deep the valleys may be, the reemergence of decency and decorum is always possible.

Once more, in Brazilian history, it is urgent for purity to manifest itself against two-faced moralism, and for translucent seriousness to shine through against the audacity of shamelessness. In order to preserve hope, it is necessary to identify also as examples of deterioration the disrespect for popular classes,the indecent salaries paid to teachers in basic education, the lack of respect for public property, the excesses of government, unemployment, destitution, and hunger. These truly constitute the pornography of our lives. And so does discrimination, be it against blacks, women, homosexuals, the indigenous, the fat, the old.

It is imperative that we maintain hope even when the harshness of reality may suggest the opposite. On this level, the struggle for hope means the denunciation, in no uncertain terms, of all abuses, schemes, and omissions. As we denounce them, we awaken in others and ourselves the need, and also the taste, for hope.

And what could education do toward hope? A gnoseologic process, education engages subjects (educators and learners), mediated by a cognizable object, or the content to be taught by the educator–subject and learned by the learner–subject. Whatever the perspective through which we appreciate authentic educational practice—gnoseologic, aesthetic, ethical, political—its process implies hope. Unhopeful educators contradict their practice. They are men and women without *address*, and without a destination. They are lost in history.

In an effort to maintain hope alive, since it is indispensable for happiness in school life, educators should always analyze the comings and goings of social reality. These are the movements that make a higher reason for hope possible.

From a historical point of view, a rigorous analysis of the facts reveals that certain events considered negative are more positive than they may seem. No matter how shocking the facts may be, the remedy could never be the closing of society once again. In reality, the negatives we experience today do not raise doubts about democracy. It is exactly because we are exercising democracy with renewed vigor that certain events are taking place and that we are becoming aware of many others.

The impeachment, for example, of a president would not have been possible if Brazil had not reached the level of political-democratic maturity it has. Only the improvement of democracy, which implies overcoming social injustice, can demonstrate how worthwhile all the hope we put into the fight was. In reality, a regime that abuses power was never an introduction to democracy. During the time since we began transitioning from authoritarianinism to democracy, in the obstacles faced, we felt the risk that hope would run out. This is a transition that is now complete, there being no reason to speak about it from now on. We now need to consolidate democracy, shore up its institutions, ensure a return to development, and ensure economic balance, with which we may face the social problems that afflict us.

In alliance with the right, we will never accomplish that.

Notes

BY ANA MARIA ARAÚJO FREIRE

Introduction

Sharing a book with Paulo Freire is both a privilege and a pleasure of mine. As his wife, I never took his invitations to participate in his work as a right or duty, but as a privilege and pleasure.

It is a privilege to contribute to his writings, and in the process make and remake myself both as an intellectual and as a Brazilian. Paulo's narrative in this book, as in the others he wrote, is taken from the day-to-day of his life, his emotions and reflections, his experiences as Recifean, Pernambucan, and Brazilian as lived out in the world. Walking down this path along with him thus makes and *remakes* me more historian and more authentically national.

It is a pleasure to know myself as sharing with him not only the daily joy of the good husband–wife relationship, but also the satisfaction of living and sharing political-pedagogical concerns which, my own previously, have become more and more *ours* in recent years.

In *Pedagogy of the Heart,* my care in producing these notes are the same with which I wrote the notes for *Pedagogy of Hope* and *Letters to Cristina.* Thus, I wish to place myself "under the shade of this mango tree"—which reflects Paulo's original Portuguese title for his book—with the privilege and pleasure of being able to enjoy Paulo's ideas and his company, since he feels more lucid and creative under this and other Northeastern trees.

These notes are not meant to invade the author's text, but to complement it. Some may perhaps seem unnecessary; however, Paulo's language and ideas go beyond the local level, leading me to translate them for a universal public. My notes intend to contextualize this text in many of its apparently obvious time, space, and Brazilian culture references. They are simply descriptions, narratives, and reflections meant to clarify, but never to interfere in the dialogue between the author and his readers.

Note 1—Page 36

In 1995, the National Conference of Bishops of Brazil (CNBB) organized its annual Fraternity Campaign on behalf of the men, women, and children whose political and economic powers have been excluded from participation in society. Through the campaign, the Catholic Church exhorted society to become aware of and engage in concrete action in favor of those historically excluded, of those less valued and left to chance.

This group includes the elderly, the disabled, the sick, the poor, street kids, sexually abused girls, the imprisoned, drug addicts, the HIV positive, prostitutes, and the unemployed. The base document for the campaign announces: "There are approximately 130,000 inmates in 297 correctional facilities, representing an excess of 2.5 inmates per space (...) five hundred thousand girls prostitute themselves on Brazilian streets (....) The youngest prostitute on record was eight years old. The traffic of underage youth and children for prostitution is alarming." According to CNBB data, 32 million people starve, 7 million suffer from physical or mental illness, and millions of children begin working prematurely. In addition, at least 500,000 people carry the HIV virus."

The Catholic Church in Brazil has, since the sixties, presented a considerably progressive segment of the clergy, completely involved with the cause of the oppressed. CNBB is one of its institutions, which had been opening space, until May 1995, with Monsignor Luciano Mendes de Almeida, not only for evangelization but also for fighting against sociopolitical injustice. Throughout the entire military period (1964–85), the outraged voices of various leaders, like Monsignor Paulo Evaristo Arns, were raised against the arbitrariness of, above all, the torturing and the vanishing of political prisoners. With the political opening, the situation of those excluded from material and cultural benefits had been the main concern of this clergy, who to a large extent led CNBB's actions. More recently, the privatizing and globalizing neoliberalism of the current president of the republic has met the repudiation of these clergymen, because they know it is impossible to integrate the excluded into this system so highly individualistic and disinclined toward social causes.

Note 2—Page 38

Freire talks about his childhood world through trees and their shades, important components of Northeastern life. He speaks about the cajú tree, a tree natural to the region of mangos, whose unique flavor can be savored in the form of juice, preserved in its natural state, or infused in cachaça to make, with the "friendly cajú," the happiness of those Sundays by the sea; the cajú fruit also yields delicious cashew nuts. He speaks, as well, of mango trees, brought by the Jesuits at the beginning of colonization, with their huge, succulent fruit that varies in color, flavor, and size. He speaks of enormous jaca trees, which offer generous pulp-enveloped seeds, and of barrigudeira trees, or paineras, enormous trees with "very thick trunks, with great water reserve, red flowers, and fruit which is a winged capsule." (Aurélio Dictionary)—its flakes are used to make soft and inexpensive pillows.

Emphasizing "colors, smells, fruits," Freire refers to the qualities of trees that, up until the fifties—before skyscrapers flooded cities with condos—filled the backyards of dwellings in any city section, regardless of the social class residing in it, and thus attracted birds. Things of a missed past. Other fruits also populate the author's memories, such as the cajá, pitanga, star-fruit, araçá, papaya, umbu, graviola, pinha, sapoti, ingá, pitomba, mangaba, guava, banana, jaboticaba, pomegranate, and pineapple . . . whose pulps and juices and ice creams to this day delight those who have not caved in to the marketing of sodas.

Note 3—Page 40

Speaking of the contradictions of "my homeland," not only the Northeast but the whole of Brazil, generous and prodigal in creative people of an exuberant nature, oftentimes watches on, not without fight, while its dominant class, endorsed by the middle tiers of society, treats millions of others with sordid contempt, condemning them to hunger, poverty, disease, and illiteracy. Freire, among so many others who fight for these people, groans with emotion and justified indignation.

Some data points to the degree of injustice in the distribution of social wealth among Brazilians. Social class in Brazil is, in great part, linked to color. Black men and women, due to a slave mentality still in existence, are looked upon as intrinsically inferior beings. Between 1531 and 1810, there are records of 6.1 million slaves entering Brazil from Angola, The Ivory Coast, Luanda, and Benguela. (By comparison, in 1810 the population of Brazil was of 4.1 million people, according to IBGE* data.) In 1990, the population of African origin reached approximately 7.2 million blacks and 57.8 million *darks*—a designation that clearly indicates a racist view—within a total of 147.3 million Brazilians.

Our colonial-patriarchal heritage leaves women, even white ones, with the smallest share of all the social wealth. There are also discrepancies in the distribution of cultural and material wealth among the different geographic regions.

The plight of pensioners and the retired is tragic: 12.3 million Social Security beneficiaries receive only minimum wages (approximately $100.00). In 1990, life expectancy was 65.49 years, 62.14 for men and 68.98 for women. In the Northeast, these numbers dropped to 60.84 and 67.74. In Suriname, one of the poorest countries in Latin America, the average life expectancy is 70 years (*Folha de São Paulo*, 3/8/95).

In 1990, out of every thousand children born alive, 51.6 died on average: a rate of 58.7 for males and 44.3 for females. In the South Region, the per thousand rates were 33.6 and 19.6, and in the Northeast they reach, for males and females respectively, 95.6 and 80.6 (IBGE, *Annual Statistics Manual of Brazil*, 1993). In Spain, the per thousand rate is six for children who die within the first year of life. In Haiti, the poorest country in the Americas, the average rate is 86 per thousand, lower than that of the Northeast (88.2 in average). In São Paulo, the chances a poor child born

---

*IBGE: Brazilian Institute of Geography and Statistics.

in the city's outskirts will die within its first year of life are 3.5 times higher than those of children born to families residing in the central areas of the city, which have better services because that is where the more privileged segments live.

Among the causes of death are "poorly defined intestinal infections"—diseases of destitution. In Brazil as a whole, such infections appear in eighth place as the cause of death; in the North, they come in second place; in the Northeast, in third; in the Southeast, twelfth place; in the South, in tenth place; in the Center-West, in ninth place.

In the past twenty years, we have become more and more a violent society, as a result of the silence imposed by the military dictatorship, which made the concentration of income easier: 80 percent of the deaths from homicide occur among youths between fifteen and eighteen years of age; of all violent deaths among children and youths (including street boys and girls), the highest rate is of homicides (31.6 percent); 31.2 percent are the result of traffic accidents; 10 percent for lack of medical assistance (recorded in Rio de Janeiro alone), and 1.6 percent are suicides (from *CBIA— Brazilian Center for Childhood and Adolescence*, published by *Folha de São Paulo*, 10/1/94).

Within an estimated population of 156.3 million for 1995, 41.9 million (26 percent of the total) are considered "poor" by the government—those without enough income to cover expenses for such basic needs as shelter, clothing, and education. From these, 16.5 are considered "destitute," for they live in extreme poverty and cannot even manage their basic nutritional needs.

The gap in standards of living between the sexes is also glaring: in 1990, the "average monthly income for persons ten years of age and older" in Brazilian cruzeiros (Cr$), was Cr$24,156.00, while for women it was Cr$8,238.00. If the women in all regions had one-third of the income of men, another datum reveals the gap between different regions. While the average income in the Northeast was Cr$8,446.00, in the North it was Cr$17,652.00; in the Southeast, Cr$19,846.00; in the South, Cr$16,452.00, and in the Center-West, Cr$18,589.00, in the years when the actual national value of minimum wages reached Cr$10,110.47.

Quasi woman-girls painfully suffer the consequences of a highly unjust society by prostituting themselves with foreign tourists. It is the so-called sex-tourism. In the hopes of marrying Europeans, a dream resulting from the fact that some such marriages do occur, whether successfully or tragically, the girls will join these tourists for fifteen-day periods, happy and submissive vacation companions. According to the Congressional Investigative Committee on Child Prostitution, there are 500,000 such girls; according to UNICEF data, there are 10 million.

In 1990, according to IBGE, the rate of illiteracy among persons seven years old and older was 10.6 percent. In the North Region it was 14.2 percent; 11.2 percent in the Southeast; 11.0 percent in the South; 17.6 percent in the Center-West, and 39.1 percent in the Northeast.

A UNICEF–IBGE study, based on 1991 data, reveals that illiteracy reaches 1.3 million Brazilians between the ages of fifteen and seventeen, or 12.4 percent of all Brazilians within this age bracket. The South and Southeast offer a better picture regarding literacy: in four Southern cities and two in São Paulo, the illiteracy rate is zero, and of the fifty Brazilian cities with rates lower than 1.5 percent, forty-nine are in these two regions. In the North and in the Northeast, confirming their inferior condition, are located all the fifty cities with illiteracy rates higher than 54 percent; in the worst cases, the rates reach 61.97 percent up to 81.23 percent. The study indicates that out of 4,491 towns, 1,500 had illiteracy rates higher than 20 percent: an alarming index, given that those who are not able to read and write by the time they are seventeen will hardly manage to learn after that (*Folha de São Paulo*, 4/22/95).

This situation is the result of a historic process of political-economic-ideological development made acute by the intensification of income concentration since 1960. In that year, the top 10 percent richest segments had income thirty-four times higher than that of the top 10 percent poorest segments. Thirty years later, the difference has jumped to 78 times higher. In 1989, on average for Latin America and the Caribbean, the top 20 percent poorest segments accounted for 4.1 percent of general income, almost twice as much as the same segment in Brazil. Still according to IBGE, the top 1 percent richest segment of the Brazilian population accounts for 13.9 percent of all income, while the top 50 percent poorest segments account for 12.1 percent; 52 percent of all workers make less than twice the minimum wage; 16.9 percent of children between ten and fourteen years of age already work; 31 percent of the elderly receive no Social Security benefits; only 12 percent of rural populations have bathroom facilities, and 4 million children are out of school (*Folha de São Paulo*, 3/8/95).

This is one of the most painful faces of a country that ranks as the eighth largest economy in the world.

Note 4—Page 42

(More information on Rural Leagues may be found in note 34, which I wrote for *Letters to Cristina*.)

Note 5—Page 45

As he speaks about Northeasterners, Freire identifies with his people not only on the basis of their lyricism, their astute intelligence, or their taste for the sun and the shade of trees and the scents that most of them exude with tropical dignity, but also on the basis of a solidarity of difference. It is the tragic difference that the living conditions in the Northeast have been making more and more marked between Freire, who for a number of reasons, was able to break free from the narrow-mindedness, apathy, immobilization, and lack of hope, and those who, still immersed in all these things, perpetuate their condition as easy preys of the "assistance and aid" that facilitates all destitution.

Having been the premier location for the Portuguese colonial-mercantile venture since the sixteenth century, the Northeast saw, as early as in the imperial era, the massive transference of its greatest wealth, sugar, overseas or to the other Brazilian provinces. The economic decadence of a region that did not orient its infrastructure toward other industries with the least bit of enterprise, not even those so-called tropical, made for the stagnation of productive social relations. Thus, historically centered in *latifundios*, the Northeast perpetuated the elitist and enslaving authoritarianism that precludes from having, being, wanting, being able, and knowing an immense rural population, even more than in the big cities. A contingent of men and women deeply rooted in a magical conception of the world easily falls prey, out of an instinct of survival, to the compassionless web of the "lords," owners of everything and everyone, and allow themselves to be "assisted" and even enslaved.

In the Northeastern *latifundios*, the order of the day is to torture and kill all workers who lead or support the struggle against exploitation. In Bahia alone, between 1979 and 1988, 138 rural worker leaders were murdered. By eliminating these liberating minds and spreading terror, the land owners intend to subjugate their victims through silence (*Ogundê*, volume 1, number 2, Savador, Bahia, 6/30/89, p. 4).

Of the 1,781 murders perpetrated against Brazilian rural workers between 1964 and 1994, "only twenty-nine cases went to trial, and in only fourteen were there convictions; the other fifteen resulted in acquittals! (. . .) The number of workers kept as slaves in different estates is a strong indicator: 40,694, between 1989 and 1993. The murderers of Chico Mendes . . . remain at large. Priests who fight for the rights of the rural are threatened with death" (Newsletter by the group Torture Never Again—Rio de Janeiro, number 16, March 1994, p. 4).

The Josué de Castro Center, in a joint study with the Save the Children Fund, announces that, "in 1994, sixty thousand children between seven and thirteen years of age labored in the heavy work of sugarcane harvesting in the plants and mills of the *Zona da Mata* area of Pernambuco (. . .). This multitude of minors represented 25 percent of the work force employed in the sugarcane harvest (. . .) the average family income in the region was a miserable $23 monthly, and the wages made by the minors would only suffice to buy 58.6 percent of the "minimum recommended ration," that is, the nourishment needed merely to replace the energy used on the job.

Fifty-six percent of these children began work at the age of seven, 57 percent hurt themselves with sickles while working in the sugarcane fields, 90 percent are hired under the table, and 100 percent of the children are recruited for a forty-four-hour work week (*Nova Escola* magazine, number 84, May 1995, p. 51).

World Bank data indicate that the "224 *latifundios* in The Northeast, each larger than 10,000 hectares, control more land, in absolute terms, than 1.7 million *minifundios* would" (in *Caminhar Juntos*, newsletter of the Juazeiro Diocese, Bahia, volume 16, number 169, December 1991, p.7).

In 1991, the rural workers' newspaper exposed the concentration of productive lands: 50 percent of them belong to 2 percent of land owners, resulting in a 70 percent exodus of the rural population, who most often find unemployment, marginalization, and hunger (*Sem-Terra*, volume 10, number 107, September 1991). The biggest land owner in Brazil owns 2.1 million hectares, an area equivalent to El Salvador (*Aeroesp Newspaper*, São Paulo, number 203, December 1994–January 1995).

Ninety thousand houses that served as homes for plant workers have been destroyed in the past four years, after the layoff of local residents, who are then reduced to *boias-frias*.* Plant owners argue that the costs associated with bringing rural workers to a par with urban workers, mandated by the 1988 Constitution, has exorbitantly increased employers' payments into Social Security. A study by the Federal University of Alagoas shows that the change in rural labor relations has contributed to the process of ghettoization, to violence, to child mortality, and to the cultural crumbling of the populations involved.

In order to convey a better sense of the magnitude of this demolition, I can give two examples: in the past twenty-nine years, the Housing Authority in Alagoas has only built 23,034 popular houses; according to IBGE, in 1991 the capital of the state had forty-nine favelas, and by 1995 this number had climbed to 120 (*Folha de São Paulo*, 5/28/95).

In the meantime, agrarian reform—needed to solve a number of national problems and particularly imperative in the Northeast, due to the miserable situation of its people, and one of the reasons for the deposition of President João Goulart in 1964—was resurrected in the democratic-transition administration of José Sarney (3/15/85–3/15/90) under the title of National Plan for Agrarian Reform. The plan served only to derail the struggle of the landless who naively gave a vote of confidence to the government, con-

---

* *Boias frias*—a term referring to the hords of destitute rural workers who have no place to go and make a living by being transported from sugarcane field to sugarcane field to work on the harvest.

cerning its promises of settlements: up until the end of the plan, in December 1989, only 10 percent of what was promised had been realized (*Ogundê*, Bahia, number 9). The Land Program during the Collor administration, which promised to settle four hundred thousand families, was forgotten; the same president allowed sugarcane plant owners to refinance their debt, shoring up the privileged situation of the exploiters.

In May 1995, immediately after the new CNBB board of directors (whose position is, in the least, conservative) took office, the present, neoliberal government of Fernando Henrique Cardoso fired the president of the National Institute of Colonization and Agrarian Reform, a man trusted by the progressive clergy, and engaged with them in the issues of the landless and of rural labor. That happened at the same time that the debt of 1,227 farmers with the Bank of Brazil was renegotiated as a function of pressure from the "ruralist caucus" in congress, which plays with its support to the reforms desired by the government.

"On the basis of an average one thousand *reais* per hectare, the government could claim back nothing less than three million hectares of land. If we take as an average fifteen hectares per family, that land would have allowed the settlement of two hundred thousand families; in other words, the entire settlement goal of the FHC administration" (*Sem Terra*, number 147, May 1995). For all these reasons, five million small land owners can no longer obtain financing from government banks and are subjected to using their land to pay the debt they incurred in order to produce.

Note 6—Page 61

Anísio Teixeira is one of the most important educators in Brazil. Born in Bahia, in 1900, the son of a very rich family, he early on dedicated himself to education. He was unable to do it his entire life because, wrongly accused of being a communist, he was pulled away from his greatest interest twice, during the *getulian* and the military dictatorships. He died at the age of seventy-one, after a lifetime committed to the cause of public education.

His extensive work and role within national public agencies (he was secretary of education in Bahia twice, and in Rio de Janeiro, then Federal District, and he directed both Capes and CNPq),* as well as international ones (UNESCO), always focused on strengthening public education and fighting elitism, submission, fear, educational centralization, and bureaucratic policies that diminish the act of educating. His guidelines were democracy and economic development through industrialization based on science and social peace, attained by citizens primarily educated by the state. Knowledge would be the result of experience, creativity, and responsibility by means of an education directed toward the future.

A man of integrity, intelligence, and tolerance toward others, but rigorous with himself, combative, not prejudiced, and enterprising, Teixeira was a follower and advocate of John Dewey's ideas. With a doctorate degree from Columbia University, he became an admirer of Dewey and the U.S., which was the reason why the Brazilian left never forgave him. During the two most authoritarian periods of Brazilian history, he suffered with accusations of being a communist, even though he was a liberal, only because his North American master influenced Krupskaya, Lenin's wife and mastermind of Russia's educational policy. Misunderstood or valued, reprimanded or exulted, Anísio Teixeira never caved in during his struggle for a more egalitarian and just Brazil.

Note 7—Page 63

The two seminars Freire refers to took place after his twenty-nine-month term heading the department of education (SME) of São Paulo, but they were inspired in his understanding of education, giving continuity to the dialogic process in the act of educating initiated by him. From the early stages of organization, dozens of meetings were held at which projects and ideas were discussed. Informational bulletins and communications were issued. The intent of the events was to share the emotion, the work, and the invention of local education. During the two-year preparation

---

*Capes: The Ministry of Education's Center for Research Support.
CNPq: National Research Council.

stage, almost fourteen thousand people debated victories and necessities of public education (Official Publication of SME-SP, p. 5).

The objectives of the First Municipal Seminar on Education—the first on record with the characteristics, dimensions, and nature of the seminar, held from October 1 to 4 in 1991—were "to broaden discussions around the political-educational principles of SME, discuss basic topics associated with national education, create another opportunity in the process of permanent development of educators, record and publicize the advances of pedagogical action in local schools, foster discussion on the diverse experiences within the different areas of public education impact in the local schools" (p. 8).

The First Seminar drew six thousand registrations—educators, school workers, parents, public school students, and guests from other institutions. It included symposiums, roundtables, practice reports, thematic discussion groups, displays of pedagogical material, and artistic events. During these sessions, day and night, participants reflected on the relationship of education to: freedom, democratization, knowledge, the educator's commitment, and the national policy on the education of children and adults. They also discussed, among other topics, elementary and basic education, interdisciplinary integration, urban planning and education, evaluation, and the issue of women as education workers. Within thematic groups, the one hundred registered schools presented suggestions about the full-day school schedule, literacy and child education, a new quality for education, the classroom, human rights and social relations, and mathematics and informatics (computers). There were presentations by art students, flute groups, choirs, dance, parades, and theater.

Ensuring the continuity of this process, from August 11 to 15, 1992, the Second Seminar was held at the Anhembi Convention Center in São Paulo. Some events were held in the area of the Centers for Educational Action (NAE's). The NAE's, ten administrative-pedagogical regions, were the base of the department of education and were implemented by Freire in substitution for the educational precincts, as dated and inadequate, a designation as the understanding of education they represented.

The event counted on the participation of seven thousand people associated with the department of education and guests from various institutions. Going deeper in the educational issue, the second seminar had as its objective debating on: education and citizenship, power relationships within the scope of the school, the role of municipal, state, and federal councils on education, experiments carried out on the state and national levels, alternative educational proposals, human rights, violence, marginalization, and the right to education.

During the various sessions, such issues as curriculum, pedagogical projects for child education, teacher development, power relations in the schools, sexual orientation, night school, the Bill of Rights of Children and Adolescents, and the new law of Guidelines and Bases for Education were discussed. Proposals of interdisciplinarity and curriculum integration were also heard and discussed. Materials produced by teachers and students were on display, such as models, books, photos, posters, artistic productions, and software. The video shows and artistic presentations represented the happy face of schools, which Paulo Freire sought to impress on the São Paulo public schools.

Two other smaller seminars deserve mention. They were held with parents and were also inspired by Freire's concept of education. He had previously held such seminars in Recife, back in the 1950s when he worked at the SESI schools. The First Municipal Parents Seminar took place on December 14, 1991, and it had the objective of strengthening the school councils and of promoting integration among parents, teachers, school workers, and students. At the end of the event, it was proposed that other such seminars be held and that Parent Development Groups and groups of school council representatives be formed.

The Second Parent Seminar took place on July 4, 1992, and had an even stronger participation of parents and educators. Among other proposals, the final document included those for: the creation of newsletters and bulletin boards for publicizing information in particular at PTA-meeting time, the creation of study groups on the rights and duties of the school community, discussions in each school about the issue of public safety, the integration of marginalized students, ample publicizing of the new School Regulations, and permanent meetings between parents and teachers (*Entre Conselhos*, November 1992).

These four events carried the Freire mark, for while already removed from the department of education, he had impressed on the São Paulo public-education system a sense of priority concerning: the democratization of the administration, a policy for the education of children and adults, the democratization of access, and renewed quality of education.

Note 8—Page 63

When Freire speaks of the voice of literacy learners in this conference organized by he and his staff at the department of education of São Paulo, he is referring not only to a fact that occurred for the first time in the history of education—an assembly where educator–learners gathered and discussed the teaching–learning process in which they were politically engaged—but also to the very speeches made by the learners themselves.

One of the strong presences was that of an approximately fifty-year-old literacy learner who married prematurely by the decision of her father, a farmer from Alagoas. A strong soul, with calloused hands and ease in communicating, the democratic leader of a community in the outskirts of São Paulo, she frequently asked the three-thousand-person audience if they wanted her to continue speaking: and they did.

She interspersed testimony about her life in the Northeast with her experience as a woman who, freeing herself from prejudice and determinations, had learned in that event something she would never have otherwise conceived of. Her knowledge was being made, produced right there and then, on December 16, 1990, in the exchange of ideas about literacy with her fellow learners and educators. She clearly understood the adversity of her illiteracy in reading and in writing, as well as all that she was acquiring through the act of discussing the present day, based on yesterday, and with hope for tomorrow. She became more politicized as she better understood herself.

She encouraged other women to seek the schools, regardless of their parents', children's, or husbands' wishes, regardless of sex, class, or age discrimination, wherever it may come from. The conference participants cheered as they felt as men and women who were making themselves citizens.

A pioneer in understanding adult education as an act of respect toward the adult's oral discourse and reading of the world acquired through years lived *in* society, and of movement toward overcoming those facts, Freire too was daring to organize an event of such a nature. He silently participated in the conference, witnessing the satisfaction of individuals who were becoming initiated in the process of knowing what they know and being able to know more. He was there as secretary of education, but also as an educator whose utopia is literacy that leads to a reading of the word and of the world.

The conference was organized by MOVA (Movement for the Literacy of Adults and Youth) and by EDA–DOT (Adult Education Program of the Directorship of Technical Orientation) in cooperation with the Forum of Popular Movements for Literacy of the City of São Paulo, made up of fifty-seven organizations. The event was meant above all to tighten the linkages among literacy learners while citizens, deepening the debate about illiteracy and its overcoming, renew the commitment between literacy learners and educators, and present the activities of MOVA and EDA learners.

Note 9—Page 80

What Freire endorses in Castanheda's interview is the agreement PSDB, a "left party," made in the elections of 1994 to elect one of its exponents for president of the republic. To that end, PSDB counted on the support of veteran politicians, from PFL (from its inception a right-wing party) and from PTB (founded in the 1940s under the inspiration of Vargas's populism and today completely removed from its ideological origins in favor of oppressed segments).

In 1989, after the defeat of its candidate Mário Covas in the first voting round of the elections, PSDB supported the then candidate of the lefts, Luiz Ignácio Lula da Silva, against Fernando Collor de Mello. In 1994, not only did PSDB enter an alliance with PFL and its mass of voters, but also it had to endorse elitist positions agglutinated under a façade of "liberal front." Even more than that, it accepted, as nominee for vice president Marco Maciel, historically a right-winger.

If the PT (Workers' Party) candidate, who had led the intention-of-vote polls since 1992, did not accept a pact with PSDB, this party did not want to take any chances and became associated with those who aspired to neoliberalism without breaking away from the neocolonialism still in place, in particular in rural areas. PSDB than was agglutinated into the coalition "Union, Work, and Progress," letting go of ideals supported by the leftist professor and intellectual Fernando Henrique, for which he was exiled in 1964.

Thus, FHC, former minister of foreign affairs and of the economy in the Itamar Franco administration, was elected on October 15, 1994, in the first round of the presidential election with 54.3 percent of the valid votes; Lula came in second, with 27.04 percent of the valid votes, defeated now no longer by an antagonist but by a former partner.

Lula's campaign had begun in April 1993, with the "Citizenship Caravans," during which he visited six hundred cities in all states to speak to the poor population, to hear it, and feel out its expectations. A perspective of victory for him was born out of the highly positive resonance of his work and out of disillusionment with Collor. However, a congressman from PSDB was able to get the Supreme Electoral Court to prohibit the use of free-TV air time for showing any images not generated in a studio. Lula, thus, lost his strongest campaign instrument: the people who attended the rallies during the caravans.

From May 1994 until the eve of the elections, Lula visited 128 cities in nineteen states and the Federal District. Cardoso had in his favor a convincing discourse in the free-TV time, the PFL forces linked to large landowners, business leaders, especially in São Paulo, and part of the middle class, who identified with his ideas and had regained its buying power of the 1970s as an immediate benefit of the Real Plan, implemented by him.

The 1994 elections divided left forces into two antagonistic groups, above all due to the ideological gap opened between them, breaking up a union forged in 1989, which had signaled a consolidated future.

During the presidential elections of 1989, the second-round dispute was between Fernando Collor de Mello (PRN) and Luiz Ignácio Lula da Silva (PT), who led the Popular Brazil Front, supported by PSDB, PDT, PCB, the progressive wing of PMDB, and PV. to Collor's New Brazil Coalition, formed by PRN, PTR, PST, and PSC, was added the support of other right-wing denominations: PL, PDS, PSD, PFL, PTB, PDC, and the conservative wing of PMDB.

The two largest unions, CUT and CGT, were in opposition to each other from the beginning of the first round; the former supported Lula and the latter endorsed Collor. Lula received non-explicit support from CNBB, even though many priests and bishops openly supported him. The press reported that members of eighty thousand ecclesiastic grassroot communities would campaign for the workers' candidate at the voting sites. The reactionary forces counted on the country's political-economic elite.

In order to lower the risk of tampering with election results, The PT set up a parallel vote-count system, with 150 personal computers manned by eight hundred people, in addition to 1.5 million election monitors. Collor's last rally was in Belo Horizonte, on December 13, 1989. Thirteen thousand people attended, according to the press, since it rained heavily. On the same day, Lula held a rally in Rio de Janeiro attended by one hundred forty-five thousand people.

On December 14 the last debate between the two candidates was broadcast by a pool of television networks from São Paulo. The program had a 79 percent viewing rating in greater São Paulo, about 12 million people, and millions of other interested viewers throughout the country. After the debate, the polls indicated a better performance by Collor (who had a 42 percent approval rate, against Lula's 27 percent). In part, these results were due to accusations by a former girlfriend of the PT candidate's that he had wanted the abortion of their daughter. Emotionally destabilized by the low hit, the workers' candidate had a hard time building his argument in the debate. And added to all that, there was a false accusation that PT was involved in the kidnapping of businessman Abílio Diniz.

Four days after the elections, the results became known: Collor won with 42.75 percent of the vote; Lula had 37.86 percent. The traps set up for the last minute, deceiving propaganda through the media, and robust campaign-financing contributions took Collor to power. Soon thereafter, the people who made him president impeached him (see notes 1, 2, and 46, *Letters to Cristina*).

Note 10—Page 91

Episodes of democratic rebelliousness, almost always accompanied by betrayal of democracy, are recorded throughout Brazilian history. Some of these movements were embedded in social struggles for utopian democratic societies; some were entirely based upon economics; they were all plentiful of conscious resistance to the established power. In most cases, they were characterized by violence, not yet extirpated from our understanding of antagonistic relations, which remains colonialistic to this day. That is especially the case in relations between those who retain power, the oppressors by "right" and the oppressed, "intrinsically inferior." Here are some of the most important rebellions in Brazilian history:

(1) The Republic of Guaranis (1610–1768), constituted by the Indians of an area including parts of Brazilian, Argentine, and Paraguayan territory, achieved social organization comparable to that described in *Utopia* by Thomas More. They manufactured fabric and musical instruments, planted, and raised animals. They had as many as three hundred inhabitants united through work, ideals, and with the aid of Jesuit priests. They were massacred in 1768, after years of resistance.

(2) Quilombos, in particular the Palmares, whose greatest leader was Zumbi (compare note 41, *Pedagogy of Hope*).

(3) The Dutch invasions in the Northeast—in Bahia (1624–25) and in Pernambuco (1630–54)—took place when the Kingdom of Portugal (and, as a result, Brazil) was subsumed by the Spanish monarchy in alliance with the Dutch. By taking over the main economic centers in the colony, they intended to recover losses incurred with the unpaid debt of landowners. When the dominant interests—those of local landowners and the Portuguese monarchy, reconstituted in 1640—opposed those of the invaders, the

resistance movement included slaves, Indians, and whites in what was termed Pernambucan Insurrection. The Dutch were only completely driven out of Pernambuco in 1654, after bloody battles. A new spirit emerged among the people then: the knowledge that united the colonized could fight against external enemies. With its prohibitions, exploitations, and punishments, Portugal was in contradiction, preparing the resistance uprisings against its domination that would take place until 1822.

(4) The Beckman Rebellion (1684) in Maranhão was the first manifestation against the commercial monopoly held by the crown. It did not have a separatist intent, nor did it hope to dispute our condition as a colony. It was led by Manuel Beckman, who, defeated, was executed by the repressive forces of the Metropolis; all other rebels were arrested.

(5) The War of Mascates (1710–14) was born from opposition between sugarcane lords who lived in Olinda, the main village in Pernambuco, and Portuguese traders who lived in Recife. The latter were creditors of Olinda's elite, and they asked King Don João V to elevate Recife to the category of village, thus entitled to having a House of Representatives. Led by Bernardo Vieira de Melo, the landowners intended to turn Pernambuco into a republic. With the rebellion defeated, the dream was over; some of them were exiled to India and Vieira de Melo died with his son in a Lisbon prison.

(6) The Bahian Inconfidence or Rebellion of Taylors (1789) took place in Salvador and was organized by intellectuals, priests, military personnel, artisans, slaves, and freed blacks. The political project of rebellion, inspired by the French Revolution, Voltaire, and Rousseau (translated by the rebels), included the constitution of a Bahian Republic, legal equality among all people, and thus the end of slavery, the end of the Portuguese monopoly on trade, and political participation for the population. Once the rebellion was dominated, some were pardoned, but those from popular classes—Luiz Gonzaga das Virgens and Lucas Dantas, João de Deus and Manoel Faustino, both mulattos like Dantas—were condemned to death by hanging. This insurrection reveals the degree of dissatisfaction and consciousness that invaded different segments of society in relation to the bloody colonial structure.

(7) The most important separatist movement, improperly called Mineira Inconfidence (1789), came about in the climax of the mining cycle as a reaction to the crown's repressive vigilance and to the legislation that expropriated the gold production. To guarantee its receipt of 20 percent of all fused gold, the crown perfected its laws more and more, until it decreed the *derrama:* in case 1,500 kilos of gold were not at the Fusing House by a certain date, the population would have to provide the remaining amount at any cost. In 1789, with the decline of mining exploration, there were 596 kilos of gold missing to complete the demanded amount, but above all, there were plenty of reasons for the insurrection. Minas Gerais intellectuals, followers of the Enlightenment, advocated then separation from Portugal, the constitution of a republic, the creation of a university in São João d'El Rei, and the development of manufacturing industry, forbidden in Brazil in 1785 by D. Maria I, among many other prohibitions. Betrayed by Joaquim Silvério dos Reis, the revolutionaries were punished with exile in Africa (some managed to obtain the king's pardon). The principal rebel, dentist Joaquim José da Silva Xavier, *Tiradentes,* had his assets confiscated and his descendants proscribed; he was hanged and dismembered, having different parts of his body displayed along public ways and his head stuck to a high pole in Vila Rica (today, Ouro Preto). The violence of such repression was opposed by a strong resistance and rebellion, which in spite of leaving deep scars of pain and broken hope, irreversibly opened the way to Brazilian emancipation.

(8) The Revolution of 1817, in Recife, was also heavily influenced by the French Enlightenment, divulged by the Olinda Seminary and by the Areópago de Itambé, a secret society devoted to the propagation of anticolonialism. Victorious in a first stage, the rebellion established a provisional republican government made up of men from the local elite, who wrote an Organic Law ensuring freedom of conscience and the press, except for attacks on the Constitution and religions (all tolerated, even though Catholicism was deemed the official religion, and its clergy was put on the state's payroll), creating a Constitutional Assembly, and abolishing taxation on products of basic necessity. The Northeastern provinces adhered. The emissary sent to Ceará was arrested, and Father Roma, sent to Bahia, was arrested and executed; others

went to the U.S., Argentina, and England, the country where Hipólito José da Costa published *Correio Braziliense*, the first Brazilian periodical. Repression came promptly: D. João VI, regent of the Portuguese Crown, personally gave instructions to the feared Count of Arches, the governor of Bahia, to contain the rebellion. Pernambuco resisted in vain. Three leaders were executed in Salvador, among whom was Father Miguelinho and three others condemned to death by hanging in Recife; the leader Domingos Teotônio Jorge was one of them. Even though the Revolution of 1817 did not claim for the end of slavery, it counted on popular support. One more time, the crown, now established in Brazil, proclaiming it the United Kingdom of Portugal and Algarves, did not lose its colonialist mark, but manifested it in bloody retaliation.

(9) The Confederation of the Equator (1821) was another episode of rebellion followed by betrayals to democracy. The frustrated aspirations of 1817 did not die. On October 5, 1821, Pernambucans expelled the governor who had crushed the rebellious movement four years earlier. Already in August, having as a leader Gervásio Pires Ferreira, former revolutionary of 1817, they had set up a provisional government, parallel to the official one, in the city of Goiana. With the country's independence in 1822, frustration increased before the absolutism of D. Pedro I, who dissolved the Constitutional Assembly. The new provisional government was dissolved by Pernambucan liberals who elected a Governing Board headed by Manoel de Carvalho Pais de Andrade, also a fighter in 1817. The fear for arbitrary measures to be taken by the recently emperor-appointed governor, and by D. Pedro I himself, led to the explosion, on July 2, 1824, of an armed movement that was named Confederation of the Equator (bringing together Pernambuco, Ceará, Rio Grande do Norte, and Paraíba). It would be a new independent state in the form of a federative republic. In order to repress the movement, the government took loans abroad and hired the naval forces of Lord Cochrane. The emperor's military troops attacked Recife and Olinda first, bringing the rebels under control. Following that, all the others were captured one by one until they got to Ceará, where the rebels capitulated on November 29, 1824. The immediate trials included atrocities. The Carmelite and popular leader Friar Caneca was

executed by gunshot because the executioners refused to pull the rope he had been sentenced to hang from. If there was the intention of autonomy in the Confederation of the Equator, that is less due to the lack of national unity, which really did not fully exist yet, than to the only possibility at that moment of making opposition to the central power, which was excessively authoritarian, discriminatory, and centralizing, very much as in colonial Brazil. Such authoritarianism had been generating historically harmful privileges and leading the dominant to combat their antagonists with cruelty so as to perpetuate the exclusion of many and the profit of few.

(10) Cabanagem (1833–39) was a revolutionary movement that took place in Pará; it was the first and only one in Brazilian history where popular segments in fact took power and ran, even if without continuity or a plan of action, the political life of an entire province. The Cabanos (a population of cabin dwellers along the margins of the Amazon rivers) felt that independence had not improved their lives and decided, with help from local leaders, to fight against the central power during the period of Regencies (1831–40). The repression operation, conducted with mercenary troops under the command of the Englishman Grenfell, responded to the first manifestations by throwing three hundred revolutionaries in the hold of a ship and filling it with chalk. With D. Pedro I's abdication in 1831, manifestations against local powers emerged once again. The Cabanos invaded Belém and executed the president of the province and other authorities. A farmer, Félix Antonio Malcher, took office as governor of Pará; however, in an unexpected turn, he declared his loyalty to the future emperor, D. Pedro II, and repressed the rebellion that had made him chief. The movement destituted and executed him. Malcher's substitute, Francisco Vinagre, also betrayed the revolutionary ideals proving to be submissive to the regency. His brother, Antonio Vinagre, became the leader, even though Francisco remained in command, and that enabled the representative of the central power to recover the government. Subsequently, Belém was surrounded by the Cabanos coming from the interior; the president of the province sought refuge, and the rebellious declared Pará an autonomous republic. The Cabanos's second government was or-

ganized by the democrat *seringueiro*,* Eduardo Nogueira Angelim, who was betrayed by his fellows. On May 13, 1836, the new president, appointed by the central power, conquered Belém and disbanded the revolutionaries, who ran away to the interior. In the three following years, they kept fighting with no results until the movement was completely eradicated. The repression left a balance of forty thousand deaths (40 percent of the population of the Grão-Pará Province).

(11) Balaiada and the Insurrection of Slaves (1838–41). In Maranhão, the free population dedicated to cattle raising enjoyed living conditions just as precarious as those of slaves. The political context, dominated by disputes between the liberal faction and the remainders of the Portuguese Liberal Party, fueled an atmosphere of dissatisfaction on the part of the less favored, above all the mixed and black segments, who clearly realized the impossibility of their social ascension. Thus, a cowboy from mixed origin, Raimundo Gomes Vieira, took over the jailhouse in the village of Manga, on December 13, 1838, leading the movement that was called Belaiada. Having great action mobility, the movement attracted sympathizers, took a significant part of Maranhão, and infiltrated all the way to Piauí, terrifying the powerful in that province. The massive slave escapes in that region, which since the eighteenth century had led to the formation of Quilombos as the only form of resistance and survival for slaves, began to add strength to the ranks of the *balaios*, especially after 1839, when they conquered the village of Caxias. Overcoming mutual differences, *balaios* and rebellious blacks agglutinated and together with some Indians were able to obtain weapons and provisions to organize a contingent of eleven thousand men. Alarmed, in 1840 the central power sent as president of the province Colonel Luis Alves de Lima e Silva, eventually given the title of Duke of Caxias. He enlisted the support of traders and land and slave owners, and organized the fight against the rebels, abandoned by the higher segments of society who feared the radicalization of the movement's popular nature. The eight thousand men in the official forces were divided in three columns and surrounded the *balaios*.

---

*Forest dwellers who make a living out of extracting latex from trees in the primitive way.

The soldiers arrested 498 women, 686 children, and after killing many slaves, returned the ones left to their owners. In 1841, the *balaio* Raimundo Gomes dissociated himself from the black leader Cosme Bento das Chagas, and with seven hundred weakened rebels and without ammunition, he surrendered. Once surrounded, Cosme was unable to regroup the movement. Already wounded, wandering, and hunted, the strong freed slave, with about two hundred *quilombers*, was arrested as he attempted to seek refuge in the jungle with Indians. His group was annihilated. Cosme called his rebellion "War of Law and Republican Freedom" and gave himself the title of "Trustee and Emperor of Freedom." He also gave himself the right to concede gifts through the Order of Rosario and to cover himself with sacred objects from the Catholic Church. Even though he was considered by Lima e Silva himself a great leader, he was tried as a ferocious killer and responsible for the black insurrection, and not as a rebel or *balaio* ally. Sentenced to death on April 5, 1842, he was hanged in September at about forty years of age. At a time when color was just as disempowered as rebelliousness, the oppressed found a common ground upon which to unite. Whites and blacks, the free and the enslaved, fought against the greater problem that affected almost all: destitution. Fighting against social injustices, such as hunger and slavery, being part of democratic rebelliousness was met with massacre and death in one's own country, just as in colonial times.

(12) The War of Farrapos or Farroupilha (1835–45) was initiated in the province of São Pedro de Rio Grande de Sul by its dominant segment without participation from the people, precluded from having any voice in the episode and summoned for the armed fight only in the capacity of providers of physical force. Gaucho cattle raisers and beef and leather traders, who supplied such products to the national exporter provinces (such as Pernambuco) and were kept from foreign markets, faced competition also from the countries in the Prata region, who were able to offer their products at lower prices in Brazil. The ranchers felt they were harmed by the official privileges given to Brazil's exporting regions; rebellious, in 1835 they proclaimed the Rio-Grandense Republic or Piratini Republic, having Bento Gonçalves as first president. Made to step down and arrested by the mercenary forces of Grenfell, he

was taken to Salvador. Subsequently, he escaped and returned to Rio Grande do Sul and reinitiated the fight of *farrapos* with help from, among others, the Italian Giuseppe Garibaldi. Garibaldi proclaimed, in Laguna (presently the state of Santa Catarina), the Catarinense Republic or Juliana Republic. In 1842, the Baron of Caxias was appointed president of that province with the mission of "pacifying it," just as he had done in Maranhão. He counted on the support of *farrapo* Bento Ribeiro, who divided the revolutionary. In March 1845 the *farrapo* leader Davi Canabarro and Caxias signed an agreement. The cease-fire was rewarded with general amnesty; *farrapo* soldiers and officers, except for generals, were engaged in the imperial army; the house of representatives was to be strengthened; taxes were lowered on products traded in the domestic market. The usual repressive tactics were not observed, obviously because there was no intention of affecting the elite.

(13) *Sabinada* (1837–38) was a middle-class movement that took place in Salvador. At the time, a law was being prepared that was interpretative of the Additional Act to the Constitution of 1824; it had a recentralizing orientation. In November 1837 the guard from the São Pedro Fort rebelled against certain political developments, and under the leadership of surgeon Francisco Sabino Álvarez da Rocha Vieira, allowed *farrapo* Bento Gonçalves, who was arrested at the fort, to escape. Sabino obtained the support of the governor's troops. The governor was forced to escape, and the Bahian Republic was instituted. Official repression counted on the support of landowners around Bahia and was characterized by the usual massacres, even with prisoners being burned alive. The "Bloody Trial" did not reserve any better fate to those who were tried later.

(14) Praieira Revolution (1848–50). The sociopolitical situation in Pernambuco was a truthful depiction of Brazil in the middle of the last century (even though in Pernambuco things were made harder due to the decline of the sugar trade, the province went from being the main one to a secondary one). On one side there were powerful landowners and foreign traders; on the other, there was a destitute mass mostly made up of slaves. Denial of those differences had already emerged in that province but it really exploded during the popular *praieiro* movement, which

sought a better world through social reform against the stifling and absolute domination represented by such figures as Rego Barros, province president, and Cavalcanti, the most powerful landowner at the time. Since 1842, the *Diário Novo* newspaper, whose printing press was on Praia Street (thus the name of the movement) brought together radical liberal politicians in combat against the conservative and their domineering and exploitative conduct. Between 1845 and 1847, the radical committed violent acts against Portuguese traders, but under the influence of utopian socialist thought they began to orient their actions toward social reform. The Pernambucan historian Amaro Quintas, in a study about Praeira ideology, emphasizes the fact that some intellectuals stood out in their role as disseminators of new European thought: the engineer and architect Vauthier, a revolutionary and builder of the Santa Isabel Theater; the geometry professor Antonio Pedro de Figueiredo, nicknamed Cousin Fusco (because he was mulatto and because of his interest in the philosopher Cousin, whose texts he translated), and who could see farther than the others as he denounced the antagonism between classes, and the flawed social organization, based on latifundios, beyond the despotism of local families; Abreu e Lima, *the general of the masses*, author of pioneer socialist works (published in 1835, before Marx's *Manifesto*) about the class conflict between free men and slaves; Antonio Borges da Fonseca, the *Repúblico*, a popular speaker and journalist, author of *Manifesto do Mundo*, of 1/1/49, signed by all *praeiro* leaders. The document demanded a Constitutional Assembly, political-administrative decentralization, free and universal vote rights, freedom of thought and press, the right to work, exclusive rights to retail for Brazilian citizens, independence between the branches of constituted power, the elimination of the Moderator Power and the right to make gifts, judiciary reform, and the elimination of conventional interest law and of the recruiting system. The two main leaders in the *Praeira* were Pedro Ivo, at the military command, and Borges da Fonseca who, at the political command, ensured a turn of the movement in the direction of social reform. On the operational level, however, rebellious forces, for the most part made up of countrymen poorly familiar with the topography of Recife, got lost in the city's labyrinth of streets, hastening their defeat. According to Amaro

Quintas, the *Praeira* was not successful because, in addition to
the lack of material resources, the popular potential was not well
oriented or effectively utilized at the appropriate moment for the
taking of power. Pedro Ivo was the only one knowledgeable of
other combats, including guerrillas. Arrested, he was sentenced
to life in prison along with other leaders. The *Praeira* was
the most real and the last of the democratic rebellions in
imperial times.

(15) The Rebellion of Canudos (1893–97) did not arise from
rebelliousness against certain segments of society; rather, its
foundation was religiousness. Denying Brazilian social structure
as a whole, the movement only became an armed conflict when
it was pushed into that by central power forces. Antoni Vicent
Mendes Maciel, a religious man who wandered around the Northeast preaching Catholicism—the Church was in a campaign to
come closer to the people—and later making opposition to exclu-
sions and running away from persecution settled, at the age of
sixty-five, on an abandoned farm in the Bahian wilderness, on the
banks of the Vaza-Barris River. He came upon an extremely poor
village where people smoked pipes over a yard long: "canudos."
He attracted followers and created a community that had up to
thirty thousand members. He became a "counselor" for the community, which was well organized from a social, political, economic, religious, and cultural point of view. The group's motto
was to work and lead an honest life in order to win the Kingdom
of God. Such a fact seemed a threat to the dominant, who began
to accuse the community and its leader of being religious fanatics
because they prophesied the end of the world for the end of the
nineteenth century. They were also accused of being extreme
monarchists because they abhorred civil marriage and the secular-
ization of cemeteries, certainly due to mystical and misinformed
readings about the nature of the republic, and since they rebelled
against taxation, were considered to be luring away workers from
neighboring farms. Finally, the community was accused of meddling in the business of the Church, the state, and of the landowners. The dominant urged the community leader to dissolve the
group, but to no avail. Faced with his resistance, they called in
the army. After three failed attempts at repression, it was only in
the fourth expedition, armed with cannons and machine guns,

that they were able to crush Canudos, on October 5, 1897, twelve days after the death of Antonio The Counselor; the community went down without surrender. In his book *Os Sertões*, author Euclides da Cunha depicted the survivors: "They were only four: an old man, two ugly men, and a child, before whom five thousand soldiers roared furiously." The setting was formed by thousands of people dead from the "stubbornness" of their faith and their hope for a better world. In a poor, small, and limited world such as the one that they had created they had all that they wanted. Not being able to or not wanting to understand them, the tyranny of the dominant eliminated them with bloody violence. The mystique of Canudos did not die: every October 5 pilgrims go to that location to pray, even though the Vaza-Barris River and the ruins of the village have been flooded by the immense Corocobó Dam.

(16) Contestado War (1912–16). The need for subsistence land and messianic religiousness led about fifty thousand rural residents from Santa Catarina and Paraná to dispute among themselves the demarcation of lands between the two states. Monks and religious laypersons adhered to the movement. One of them, José Maria, considered to be the reincarnation of monk João Maria because he had the same habits and because both became involved in the fight for land, died in a confrontation alongside the countrymen. This fact was taken as a divine sign that they should abandon the fight for the land and unite. They believed that their religious leaders, who advocated the end of the republic and the return of monarchy, at which time the "army of Saint Sebastian" and that of the countrymen killed would return and defeat the forces of evil. The official troops attacked by land and by air (airplanes were used against the country's population for the first time in Brazilian history) allied with the police and hired killers. These troops, acting in the name of the "threatened republic," served the interests of local landowners and colonizing companies. They attacked the core of the rebellion, the "holy villages," until they were destroyed in 1916, killing thousands of country folks whose only error was to believe in a monarchy that would bring them the happiness of heaven and land to live on.

(17) The Caldeirão experiment (1922–31), located in the back lands of Ceará, was conducted by Priest Cícero Romão Batista, the revered *Padim Ciço*. He turned his farm over to a religious

man, José Lourenço, so that he would run it. At that location, an area of approximately 1,200 hectares in Juazeiro, the religious man founded the Order of Penitents, whose motto was faith-work-cooperation. Production was plentiful, but the fear and the greed on the part of *latifundio* owners was greater. Priest Cícero, the owner of land and buildings, and mentor of the order, already excommunicated from the Catholic Church due to his unorthodox ecclesiastic practices, a political leader who made opposition to dominant persons and interests, served as a good excuse for the bishop in the next rival town, Crato, to support the attack by conservative forces to the Caldeirão Community. Reactionary forces applauded police action; led by Captain Bezerra, they set fire to four hundred cabins leaving about two thousand people without shelter. The community moved to a different location with six hundred cabins and three thousand people, who, more cautious, began to bury their provisions. A new joint action on the part of the army and the police, in which three airplanes were used, crushed the community. The total balance was four hundred deaths, including sixteen children. One more small religious community massacred, destroyed by forces of the power established to defend the interests of the dominant. Dreams of freedom were crushed so that archaic and unjust forms of colonialist social organization could remain. Today's social movements seeking land for agriculture have been repressed with the same violence recorded in previous centuries. The Country Leagues of the 1950s and 1960s reappeared in the 1980s with the Movement of Landless Rural Workers (MST), and they were more successful than all previous movements since they did obtain some settlements. The murder of *seringueiro* (rubber extractor) leader Chico Mendes, committed at the end of 1988 by farmers, added his name to a list of many other union leaders who were hit by the secular extermination of the oppressed in Brazilian society. It is as if we were still living in colonial times, when killing and massacring were legal rights of those under the tutelage of the metropolis.

(Bibliography: CALADO, Alder Julio F., *Rethinking the 500 Years*, João Pessoa, Idéia, 1994; QUINTAS, Amaro, *The Social Sentiment in the Praeira Revolution*, Recife, Oficinas Gráficas da Imprensa Official, 1946; ALENCAR, Francisco et al., *History of*

Brazilian Society, Rio de Janeiro, Ao Livro Técnico, 1981;
KOSHIBA, Luiz and PEREIRA, Denise, *Brazilian History*, São
Paulo, Atual, 1979; SANTOS, Maria Januária Vilela, *Balaiada and
the Insurrection of Slaves in Maranhão*, São Paulo, Ática, 1983;
COSTA, Nicola S., *Canudos: Order and Progress in the Backlands*, São Paulo, Moderna, 1990; BASBAUM, Leôncio, *History in
the Backlands*, volume 2, São Paulo, Alfa-Ômega, 1975.)

Note 11—Page 98

This reference leads me to Marília Fonseca's research on contracts
between the Brazilian government and the World Bank. She built
her dissertation based on documents, some confidential, kept at
the bank's headquarters in Washington; receipts for payments
made to the Brazilian Treasury Department, letters from cabinet
members, and recorded interviews with technicians from the
bank. Segments of these contracts depict the World Bank's expro-
priation of Brazil:

> In general each contract ends up costing Brazil three
> times its original value. Also, another important aspect
> is not discussed; that is, the return of this investment in
> pedagogical terms. . . . The projects failed . . . when crite-
> ria were adopted which met the objectives set by the
> World Bank and by the Brazilian government. *Schools
> do not improve. Teachers, who should be trained, still
> demonstrate the same deficiencies as before. Student
> performance also remained the same* [my italic]. Over
> twenty years, the World Bank invested $100 million in
> educational projects in Brazil. The Brazilian government
> itself spent $217 million on the same projects and has
> incredibly high debt, of another $80 million. Not to men-
> tion the servicing of this debt. One cannot say that spend-
> ing $280 million in order to receive $100 million is a
> good deal.

I agree with the author who says that the World Bank "is not a
charitable organization . . . it is a superpower," whose financing

logic is incompatible with social investment; that it has clear political orientation toward intervention in creditor countries, given that it is paid for by the countries in control of the international economy; that its demands and conditions are less advantageous than those of landing banks in general (0.75 percent a year over the reserved amount, which is paid out after a year, when the creditor country receives reimbursement, plus 0.5 percent as payment for the funds raised). For conscious politicians and educators, the World Bank represents an undeniable political and economic threat (*Veja* magazine, 12/23/94).

Note 12—Page 98

Disrespect for teachers and education is indeed historical in Brazil. Back in colonial times, schools were private; they belonged to the Jesuits, thus being religious schools, and only clergymen could teach in them. These clergymen having made vows of obedience and poverty, their mission was considered to be transmitting knowledge always for the glory of Christ and the Catholic Church. Education was valued in Jesuit terms, disassociated from local reality, tied to the Ratio Studiorum, the educational code implemented by all Jesuit schools around the world (it was in effect in Brazil between 1599 and 1759), and if a priest did not receive any financial reward for his teaching, he did not feel disrespected in his condition as a teacher, for he believed there to be ecclesiastical and divine rewards that were the truly important ones for him.

Starting from the Jesuit expulsion in 1759, schools became secular, public or private, and both education and teachers—who were mistakenly taken as priests of knowledge, as the image of the "soldiers of Christ," and eventually due to principles of law— have been suffering with the lack of interest, seriousness, and justice that they receive from the powers of the state and from many of those chartered for education.

With the expulsion of the Jesuits, Brazil went schoolless for thirteen years. There came "loose schools," which followed the Jesuit's educational programs, and which offered no systematization of knowledge with improvised teachers. All the euphoria with the arrival of the Portuguese Royal Family (an entourage of fifteen thousand people), followed by some "cultural creations"— the opening of higher education programs specializing in such areas of knowledge as engineering and medicine, and the transplantation of the National Library from the metropolis—was not enough to reverse the educational picture in the colony.

Note 13—Page 106

(For more details concerning "chacina da candelária," see note 2 in *Letters to Cristina*, where I add more information.)

We cannot close our eyes and our hearts to the present, permanent, and generalized violence that is sadly affecting Brazilian society; by acknowledging and understanding it, we will have the capacity to overcome it. Violent deaths in Brazil happen most among the youths across all social classes; among the upper and middle classes we witness many deaths due to the high speed of cars in the major cities of the country. The most cruel deaths, which are linked to meanness, are always committed among lower classes and between lower classes and the police.

On March 4, 1995, the nation witnessed, via television, the most perverse execution of a "marginalized" youth. The television filming crew was going to tape a report in a shopping center in Rio de Janeiro when three assailants entered shooting. The police arrived when the assailants were leaving. One escaped, the other we saw dead lying on the ground where a large number of people gathered in silence. The third assailant, who was in his twenties, was televised on the lot ground. He had been hit by a police bullet. He was later dragged to the other side of the car that was used in the hold up.

Away from the TV viewers, but not from the large number of people on the street, the wounded youth's body was hit by three more bullets. Shortly afterward, a policeman stated that, according to him, the youth had threatened him. Both international and national human-rights organizations protested this cold execution. Six months later, these policemen were found guilty.

Countries that were colonized by the Europeans in America and in Africa—because of their colonization—today remain reduced to third-world status through which they reproduce the same violence that the colonizers used to subjugate and kill the national population. Even though we have broken the yoke of colonialism, we have not been able to overcome the day-to-day killings by those in power against the dispossessed classes that are labeled by the ruling class as *outlaws* and *marginals*. In truth, these so-called outlaws and marginals are excluded from the system and are forbidden to have knowledge, desires, power, and to be fully human in our societies.

Also by Paulo Freire from Continuum

Pedagogy of Hope
Reliving *Pedagogy of the Oppressed*

This is the eagerly awaited sequel to *Pedagogy of the Oppressed*, in which Freire reflects on the impact his writings have made over the past twenty-five years. *Pedagogy of Hope* represents a chronicle and synthesis of the ongoing social struggles of Latin America and the Third World since the landmark publication of *Pedagogy of the Oppressed*.

With *Pedagogy of Hope*, Freire once again explores his best-known analytical themes with even deeper understanding and a greater wisdom. Certainly, all of these themes have to be analyzed as elements of a body of critical, liberationist pedagogy. In this book, the reader comes to understand Freire's thinking even better, through the critical seriousness, humanistic objectivity, and engaged subjectivity which, as in all of Freire's books, are wedded to a unique creative innovativeness.

"A powerful, scholarly defense of the radical liberal position." —*Choice*

Pedagogy of the City

This unique book describes the everyday struggles, political as well as administrative, fought in the urban schools of São Paulo. Its forthright examination of urban education has many applications for schools in the U.S.

"Just as unrelenting and visionary [as *Pedagogy of the Oppressed*]. It is all the more powerful precisely because Freire is not speaking theoretically."
—*The Other Side*

Pedagogy of the Oppressed
New Revised 20th-Anniversary Edition

More than 600,000 sold worldwide. "Brilliant methodology of a highly charged and politically provocative character." —JONATHAN KOZOL

Education for Critical Consciousness

Two important studies are brought together for the first time. The book comes out of Freire's innovative work in the field of adult literacy in Brazil and his studies of the practice of "agricultural extension" in Chile.

These volumes are available at your bookstore, or may be ordered from the publisher:

Continuum
370 Lexington Avenue
New York, NY 10017